T0350094

The search for principles in an unprincipled age

T H E

PROPHET

OF THE NEW MILLENNIUM

GREGORY DARK

Copyright © 2005 O Books
O Books is an imprint of John Hunt Publishing Ltd.,
The Bothy, Deershot Lodge, Park Lane,
Ropley, Hants, SO24 0BE, UK
office@johnhunt-publishing.com, www.O-books.net

Distribution in:

UK: Orca Book Services,
orders@orcabookservices.co.uk
Tel: 01202 665432 Fax: 01202 666219 Int. code (44)

USA and Canada: NBN
custserv@nbnbooks.com
Tel: 1 800 462 6420 Fax: 1 800 338 4550

Australia: Brumby Books
sales@brumbybooks.com
Tel: 61 3 9761 5535 Fax: 61 3 9761 7095

New Zealand: Peaceful Living
books@peaceful-living.co.nz
Tel: 64 7 57 18105 Fax: 64 7 57 18513

Singapore: STP
davidbuckland@tlp.com.sg
Tel: 65 6276 Fax: 65 6276 7119

South Africa: Alternative Books
altbook@global.co.za
Tel: 27 011 792 7730 Fax: 27 011 972 7787

Text: © 2005 Gregory Dark

Design: BookDesign™, London

ISBN 1 905047 57 6

A CIP catalogue record for this book is available from the British
Library.

Printed in the USA by Maple-Vail Manufacturing Group

The search for principles in an unprincipled age

THE
PROPHET
OF THE NEW MILLENNIUM

GREGORY DARK

BOOKS

WINCHESTER UK
NEW YORK USA

DEDICATION

To **Lyubov**: friend, teacher, inspiration – delight.

ACKNOWLEDGEMENTS

Rajendra Sharma introduced me to 'The Prophet'. Without that introduction, this book could never have happened. It is for that reason I separate him from the list that follows. It is only one of the debts that I owe him.

Without exception, to all those below I also owe more than one debt. There is no way to quantify their contributions either to this book or my life generally. The help of some has been momentous and on-going. That of others may have been more fleeting, but was nevertheless essential.

Without any of these people (and of others who have preferred to remain anonymous), the book would not have been what it is; without some of them, the book – simply – would not have been. My most heartfelt thanks to:

Julie Baines; Catherine Barry; Judith Browder; Brie Burkeman; Bruce Crowther; Julian Day; Graham & Sandra Easton; Hanne Elmose; Lykke Elmose Asmussen; Malachy Farren; Sheila & Willie Fonfe; Victoria Garcia Giraldo; Trish Hollingsworth & Patrick Udale; Clara Izurieta; Jill James & Ewart Needham; Gill Jones; Sarah London; Kay Lyons; Sarah Maur-Thorp; Maureen McAthey; Teresa Parrot; Joa Reinelt & Ray Villis; John Reiss; Caroline Roberts; Sue Rogers; Susan Rosen; Sally Shuter; Peter Sherlock; Bob Smith; Diana Talbot; and Andrew & Judy Wood.

Sadly, the following have died. The help they continue to provide to me has not:

Nigel Ashley; John Cannon; Elizabeth Ferwerda; Catherine O'Brien; Ann Pool; (another) Bob Smith; and Bill Wilson.

Lastly, I would like to thank my parents, step-parents and the rest of my family – those members of it who supported my endeavours, those who didn't and those who discouraged them. All these factions proved to be helpful.

Gregory Dark, London, October 2005

THE sun shone. It gave sparkle to the dimples of the sea. The boat was but a white speck in a world of blues. He knew the boat was his.

He knew it was time for him to go. Again. He saw again the citizens leave their work that they may bid him their farewells and that they may hear him once again before he went.

His heart was heavy at his departure. It was always heavy when departing.

He smiled ruefully to himself. Before he was a prophet he was a man. It behove him to remember that.

Soon a crowd had gathered.

He knew, if he were to speak to them as a crowd, he would not be speaking to them.

He looked on the crowd's faces. He saw that some loved him and that love cheered him. He saw too that a few hated him. For them his heart ached.

Hatred's first target is always its harbinger. It is only those who hate themselves who cannot weep for those who hate themselves. Their cruelty starts with cruelty to themselves.

"Citizens of Orphalese," the prophet told them. "My predecessor, Almustafa, said he would return. I, Arkona, am before you.

"Before many crowds have I spoken. But most crowds have only dissembled hearing. As a siren Orphalese pulled me to her shores, and as a limpet I have clung to them. Because here I have discovered a wisdom sufficient to hearing.

"Elsewhere the crowds are but throngs of speakers whose voices have been stilled for the moment. Even when their tongues are still, though, they chatter more than they listen.

"In Orphalese you do listen. You have the *wisdom* to listen. Listening requires so much more wisdom than speaking.

"You citizens of Orphalese, you are the wisest listeners.

"The wisest listeners hear not with their ears alone but with their heart as well and with their soul.

"The wisest do not listen to the words, and pick at them like the pan-handler scratching at the scree for the elusive nugget. They penetrate through to the spirit of the words like the sculptor who already within the slab of stone sees the final figure. And who knows no other sculptor will see the same figure – that truth demands that. And that truth makes no value judgements between the different figures seen by different sculptors in the same slab of stone.

"The wisest do not exalt in the epiphany of a moment, but allow truth rather to possess them slowly. That it may thoroughly possess them.

"The wisest do not seek answers. They seek only questions leading to further questions. The wisest have come to understand that it is not in answers but in questions that truth is nestling.

"Those unskilled in hearing will hear me talk in statements. You people of Orphalese who hearken to me with clean ears and a spirit unfettered, you will not even hear questions. You will stumble on signposts, tenuous and homespun signposts, that will lead each one of you to the questions you, each one of you, need ask yourselves. Sometimes those signposts will point at the same time in both directions. And sometimes you will try to follow both directions at once and wonder that you stay where you are.

"The wisest know, sometimes the best way forward is to wait for the signpost to change direction.

"There will be those who deride my words. Some of those will not have heard them correctly. Into the mouths of those we dislike we place the words we feel they would say. If we criticise such words, it is not their mouths that we censure but our own ears.

"My critics are frightened. But their fear of me is as nothing against the fear they have of their own noiseless quiet, the quiet to which I would urge them that they lead themselves.

"When my critics seek to misinform you, people of Orphalese, hear again what it was I did say. Go again into the noiseless quiet and have the courage to listen to what that quiet tells you. And have the courage to hear that quiet. And to heed it.

"Let your own questions form themselves.

"In the quiet you will find love. Also for those deriders: They will have widened your truth, or underscored your truth, or brought you to another truth, or cleared your ears to have allowed you to hear the truth indeed.

"Those who maintain they hear me and that they take umbrage at my words have not heard me. I preach nothing, other than that you allow your own quiet to be your own preacher. I advocate nothing, other than that your own quiet be your own judge.

"I urge only that you have a happier life.

"If I do offend it is because you are disturbed not by me, not even by yourself, but by your perception of yourself distorted by the noise. And by a perception, likewise distorted, of your own best interests and your own happiness."

The prophet started to walk a little way amongst them.

"People of Orphalese," he said, "yours is an awesome destiny.

"We live in terrible and dangerous times. You who are listeners, you must teach the world to listen. To listen as you listen. With wisdom, with its heart and with its soul. For it not to listen will be for the world to die.

"And it must listen not to the talkers but to the streams crying acid tears and to the forests dying by a thousand cuts, to the shrieks of orphans suckling at hollow breasts and to the thunder of hollow bellies, to the screams of those hit by bullies and by bullets.

"Speakers – so many speakers – speak only that we will not hear those sounds, the sounds of truth. They fear for the consequences to themselves. They think true happiness reeks of unhappiness, and that surrogate happiness is better than none. Which is sad for them, but toxic when that fear is moulded into creed.

"Real listeners revel in the noiseless quiet. It is so often in such quiet – and only in such quiet – that we truly hear, and that we hear truly."

●●●

THERE was a child in the crowd. Eight-years-old. Her hair was so brown it was almost black. It had been cropped short. Her dark brown eyes shone with great humour and with the wisdom of artlessness.

"Noiseless quiet?" she asked. "To have a noiseless quiet you'd have to have a noisy one. And you can't have a noisy quiet. That's silly. Everyone knows *that*."

He loved this child. Her name, he knew, was Saskja. She reminded him of his children when they had been her age: pert, precocious, impudent, impish. He squatted before her.

"If you want to know what a miracle is, this is a miracle," the prophet said. "A child, any child, is a thing so wondrous that even history's most gifted poet can only hint at its wonder.

"When we glory in a child because he is our future we glory in only half of a child. Children are also owners of the moment. If ever we wonder whether the emperor is clothed we need only ask a child. And if there is no child we need only find the honesty to ask the child within ourselves."

Then he turned to address the girl herself. "We create so much noise," said Arkona, "that even when we stop creating it, the noise continues for a time to echo around us. Much of that noise is created in our own heads. That noise needs stilling. Much is created by those who love us seeking to guide us. And the love needs to be acknowledged whilst that noise too is stilled. Some is the ever more raucous cacophony of life. Neither inevitability, however, nor ubiquitousness nor mundanity precludes the need to address a cause of our disturbance.

"And some of the din is the brouhaha of the cynical and manipulative who seek to keep us from our truth by deluging us with a permanent barrage, the content of which is less important than its volume.

"When we first cease allowing noise around us, the quiet we enter is still infested with noise. It is *that*, the noisy quiet you think cannot exist. A noisy quiet may well be more wholesome than no quiet, but it cannot substitute for a noiseless quiet.

"If you are thirsty enough you will drink from a muddy puddle. That does not make the puddle a spring. Nor is drinking from it the same experience as drinking from a spring.

"The noise seeks to convince us the muddy puddle is a spring.

"The quiet tells us that what the world drinks from today is infinitely more contaminated than a muddy puddle. In the noiseless quiet we start, maybe, to become aware of that.

THERE was a novice nun in the crowd who had travelled to Orphalese from Syracuse. Her grey eyes burned with a passion to know her spirit better, her young skin yearned for the wisdom wrapped in wrinkles. And the prophet loved her for her youth and for her fire, and because, lined, she would yearn for the spontaneity of a lineless face.

"Master," she said, "talk to me of God."

"I am no master," he said to her. "I am a man. With all of a man's frailties. Whatever else I am.

"Some of you believe I am Almustafa; some that I am partly he. Some believe I have ingested his spirit; some that I have absorbed that spirit as I have absorbed Shakespeare's spirit and Caesar's and Shiva's; some that we all have absorbed those spirits. All of you are right in your beliefs. That is one of the great truths, and part of the great truth.

"Whatever I am, I speak not to disseminate wisdom but to receive it.

"She who would insist you listen only to her knowledge has nothing worth the knowing.

"The greater our knowledge, the greater only our knowledge of our ignorance. Such knowledge can be imparted only with the humility to recognise nothing else can happen to it beyond it being tendered – its receipt cannot be guaranteed.

"I do not teach.

"I invite you into your own – yes, noiseless – quiet. I invite you to meander through a labyrinth of confusion. One from which only those determined to be decisive will emerge.

"There is no one more confused than she who must be decisive.

"There is no surer sign of error than an insistence one is right.

"The invitation into the labyrinth contains a real gift. That gift is yours for the accepting of that invitation. And for the conferring of it on yourselves: Only you *can* confer it on yourselves.

"The gift is not resolution. That, if it is within the province of anything, can only be within God's.

"The gift is finding your own sense within confusion and your own order within chaos.

"The gift is in the rejoicing both in the confusion and in your own sense within it, in both the chaos and your own order.

"Many of the noise-makers seem to enjoy a bumpless ride on a magic carpet. They clamour loudly,

'Look at us. We are the chosen ones. We have the gift. Look at us some more. And follow us. There is no confusion in our lives. There is only certainty. And the certainty of success. And the certainty which *is* success.'

"When we believe these noise-makers we are Aladdin swapping his magic lamp for a virtual one. We swap the miraculous for the gaudy, the genuinely special for the specious.

"To choose sureness over confusion is to choose the desert over the garden, it is to prefer despotism to free elections. It is to choose discontent before happiness, and self-deception before self-love.

"If your happiness is not humanity's happiness you are not truly happy. You are bronzed with a suntan that comes from the bottle. The mirror may lie to you, but your soul will tire of believing it.

"The true gift is hacking blindly through a jungle of quicksands and poison ivies. The true gift is the awareness that such is paradise indeed.

"It is awareness that Paradise is not ours for the taking but ours for the giving away.

"We enter Eden by standing aside that others may enter into it; we savour the fruits of paradise by presenting them to others.

"It is only when we recognise that Paradise is every man's that Everyman can enjoy it.

"God did not expel humankind from Eden. Humankind expelled itself. Each day we expel ourselves.

"We expel ourselves from Eden when we seek to keep others out of it. We expel ourselves when we cheat ourselves and we cheat ourselves when we deny ourselves our truth.

"Eden is not a never-never land outside ourselves, but an ever-ever land within ourselves.

"There is no exile more absolute than feeling abroad at home.

"We are never further from Eden than when we do not recognise we are within it."

●●●

FROM the sanctuary a little time before had come a woman who was not Almitra but Lakshmi. As Almitra had been, Lakshmi was a seeress. She had spent many hours with the prophet and knew him well, and knew herself wiser for the knowing of him.

She stood now, and waited a moment before she spoke. Her smile danced on the throng like sunflowers bending with the breeze.

Eventually she said, "I know you must go. I know your ship comes to bear you away. And I rejoice for you in your homecoming as I grieve already for your absence."

Arkona looked on Lakshmi with great love. She had always been kind to him. He knew himself to be wiser and kinder for the knowing of her. Their times together had been times of peace, watching the ever-changing sea, gazing at the stars.

"The novice asked you about God," she said to him.

"God?" the prophet asked. "We mortals cannot know God.

"But we cannot unknow God.

"We *can* know God is. The more we know God is, the less becomes our need to know God.

"Those who would know God are those who do not know God is.

"God is unknowable.

"When we talk of God being omniscient or omnipotent, for instance, we are trying to know God. We are trying to put a face on the wind.

"God operates in a sphere where considerations of omniscience or omnipotence do not apply. You are expecting the gazelle to build dams or the otter to fly.

"If you would know God, strive with all of your might not to know God. Petition to God not to know God.

"Of those who would introduce you to their God, or who would explain God to you, ask: 'Is your God a statement or a question?'

"'Is your God yours or everyone's'?

"For God to be God, God must be your God.

"A part of your God can only be found within you, just as a part of my God can be found only within me. My fingerprints may be similar to another's, they are never the same. As with the body, so the soul.

"When my brother and I look upon the earthly man who sired us we see different men. My eyes are not my brother's eyes, nor can my brother's eyes be mine. *My* father cannot be my brother's father.

"If we all have different fathers, who are tangible and visible and undeniable, how much more must we all have different Gods?

"And if it is God, the only part of God you can ever know is that part of God contained within *you*. And the only *knowledge* you can have of God is that.

"If you think you have a wider knowledge than that of God, return into the quiet. Maybe the statement is seeking to strangle the question.

"There is no universal truth, people of Orphalese. There is not even a universal question.

"Because you are allergic to tomatoes does not mean that tomatoes are poisonous. But that tomatoes are innocuous to most does not mean that they are not toxic to a few.

"As with the body so the soul.

"One of the true miracles of life is life's individuality. In the whole history of our planet with its countless petals, never has there been two identical. That is truly a miracle. Not two identical petals, nor potatoes. Not even pebbles.

"We try to apply universal laws or metaphysical laws to entities one of whose most obvious features is their separateness. We seek universal solutions to conundra – us – whose principle beauty lies in our uniqueness.

"The triumph of each life is to find that uniqueness. And to nurture it.

"Such is a life devoted to God and blessed by God."

•••

"YOU avoid pronouns when you talk of God," said a man, a schoolteacher. He was fit, the man, and sturdy. Short blond hair crowned a face younger than its years. Turquoise eyes squinted into the shimmering orchard before them.

"If you give a pronoun to God," Arkona said, "you start to define God. If you start to define God, whatever it is you are defining can no longer be God. I mean no disrespect, nor do I imply that God is necessarily inanimate if I give God the pronoun 'it'.

"My God is – my God must be – both male and female. And neuter. And abstract. Because my God is all. Which, of course, also means that my God is nothing.

"Others have a God who is only male or only female. Some, a God which is entirely abstract. For entire societies and cultures God is Gods. For the atheist, God is a non-God or an un-God or an anti-God. Most non-Gods and un-Gods and anti-Gods still are God.

"Nothing is more divided than God. But nothing is more whole.

"The divisiveness, however, which humankind accuses God of creating, is not God's handiwork at all, but that of humankind itself. Much of humankind apparently finds itself unable to cope with the notion that God's wholeness comes only from the cohesion of God's own dividedness."

The prophet plucked an apricot from the tree and handed it to a ragamuffin lolloping grimily in the earth.

"The noise-makers teach us that God is a subject for specialists. That therefore only specialists may pronounce on God. Is air a field for specialists? And because – certainly – there are some specialists in air, does that stop the rest of us from breathing?

"It is in many ways that God is like air.

"Like air, humankind has a need for God. There is no tribe so primitive but that it doesn't have its own totem and its own pantheon. There is no atheist so confirmed that at some point she has not personalised her God as she wailed into the night, 'God, if you are there, help me through this crisis.'"

The prophet stopped to smile at a child asleep in his mother's arms. He smiled at the child and then at her mother.

"But it is not for that reason that God exists," the prophet said. "God does not exist because we mortals have a need for God to exist.

"God is not there for a reason.

"God is because God is.

"To find a reason for God is akin to wanting to know God – the search for it will take you further away than ever from your target.

"To find a reason for God is to find an excuse for God. And God no more needs an excuse than God needs a reason.

"We do not seek excuses for the sun. Without the sun there would be no life. That is a fact which transcends reason.

"And the sun too, that can only be a part of God."

•••

THERE was a priest, lined with walnut wrinkles, and who beamed a toothless grin from which violets had robbed their scent. And he said, "Talk to us of prayer."

The prophet replied, "What is prayer? Listen to the quiet, and let the quiet tell you what prayer is."

A hush floated amongst them. The cicadas strummed and the birds sang; a gentle breeze rustled the leaves and lizards scuttled through the grass. And he allowed the hush to flow over them and into them, he allowed the hush to flow through them and for it to be absorbed by them, even as they were absorbing the rays of the sun.

"So often," the prophet said in a voice clanging with stillness, "we say 'prayer' and mean 'petition' or 'supplication'.

"There is nothing wrong with supplication, but it is not prayer.

"And when it is supplication, we fail to use it. We have a violin in our hands and use it as wood to kindle a bonfire.

"There are few of us wise enough to recognise that the succour sought from petition comes largely with its very articulation.

"The act of petition already eases the reeling from the blow. Often its articulation is its own answer.

"We petition God to help us, yet believe God helps us only when God *obeys* us. When God supplies God's own solutions, we curse It.

"Our prayers are most mercifully answered not by staunching the bleeding but by exposing the wound.

"Petition, in seeking something from God, is also seeking separateness from God.

"Prayer, true prayer, is a veneration of our union with God. It is a celebration of the fact that you are a part of God just as much as that God is a part of you.

"When we ask of God, we seek to thrust from us that part of God which is a part of us. We do not need to enjoin the hand to protect our eyes from the sun. The hand knows itself to be of the same body as the eyes. It will protect the eyes instinctively. It would find it nigh impossible *not* to protect the eyes.

"When we petition God we are asking the hand not to protect the eyes.

"To most real prayer words are a handicap.

"We pray most fervently when we smell a flower or when we stroke a cat or when we glory in an act of kindness.

"We pray most beautifully when we acknowledge to God the beauty both of our food and our hunger, when we recognise before God the interdependence of pain and pleasure.

"We pray most devotedly when we thank God also for our woe. For it is then we are presented with ourselves.

"We pray most deeply when we weep for the unhappy or give food to the hungry or touch the untouchable.

"We pray most effectively when we stay the hand of the torturer or sheathe our swords in the face of our enemy."

•••

AND a young man in the crowd stood up. He hadn't shaved that morning and he waggled a eucalyptus leaf between his lips. With a swagger to his girlfriend, he said: "Talk to us of the future."

The prophet said, "Shhh! Listen to the quiet. The quiet will tell you of your future, will tell you too about the threat to the lack of it. Listen only to the noiseless quiet.

"If the future of the world would be vouchsafed, let each person spend some time each day in quiet. The world would then hear all the voices that the speakers drown.

"And if you would vouchsafe your own future, then spend some time each day in your own quiet. The heart too speaks in tiny whispers and intuition needs quiet that it may hear them.

"To find your own quiet is a task harder than any of Hercules: To still the tornado within us of squabbles and of carping, of exhortation and exigency. Its reward is not in the done but in the doing.

"You think I am a prophet and that prophets see the future.

"I am not a prophet. I am not even a seer. I am a man. All I can do is to *strive* to see. My eyes are human eyes. Human eyes are restricted by horizons. Only your sight is your sight. Narcissus looking into a lake does not see the same thing as an angler or a botanist or a geologist.

"The only future I can see is the future I can see.

"Yours is that contained by your own quiet. If you want a fortune-teller, go not into a booth at the fairground, but into your own quiet. Clairvoyance is only a translation of clear sight. Only the quiet can clear your sight. Look not into a crystal bowl but into the present. Tomorrow whistles the tune composed by today.

"My quiet tells me that, if there is to be a future, the present must be seized and must be severed from its bloodied past – the violence of its antique history, and the even greater violence of yesterday's.

"God in that yesterday has been but Mammon wearing a virtual halo. Mammon is not interested in your discovering your potential. Mammon seeks only that you acquiesce in your own subjugation.

"Look to the quiet.

"Look to the love which is God. Your God. Not a God which is an alias for Mammon, nor yet a God an alibi for madmen, but your God. Your ineffable, ineffably beautiful, ineffably sane God.

"And look not to the past only of your parents but of your ancestors also.

"Look not to what the churches have said, but to what the prophets have said, the buddhas and the bodisatttvas, the masters, the shamans and the gurus. Look too beyond what these enlightened ones have said. Not even their God can be yours. And their words too were reported by scribes with vested interests and heard with ears of human fallibility. Look beyond the words to that quiet where their words will have led you.

"Look into your own quiet.

"Do not listen to me. Look into your own quiet. Listen to it. Hear it. Heed it.

"If you would have God intercede in your future, look first to that part of God which is a part of you. When you find that part, you will know your future has already been protected, that your eyes will not be allowed to smart before the sun.

"And you will know your triumph is secure.

"Because the person who knows himself and knows of the existence of God cannot be vanquished. It is not possible for such a one to do anything but triumph. Because it is precisely that which *is* triumph."

•••

A child spoke from the crowd. She had light brown hair, ringletted around two dimpled cheeks. Her saucer eyes looked about her with beguiling curiosity and a curious guile. A simple shift of orange cotton hung from bouncing shoulders.

"And what of school?" the child asked.

"The Christ," the prophet said, dropping his voice a notch in respect, "talked of foundations. On sand or stone. If the foundation of an education is not built on the stone of love, the structure will always be faulty.

"If a child's first lesson is that she is loved, her journey into knowledge and understanding and wisdom will be one, whatever the hazards, where the hyacinths are always visible.

"If a child's first lesson is that she is loved, in later life she will come to understand, and easily, that even in quicksand she is in paradise. Because she will know herself to be surrounded with vines which can enable her escape.

"If a child's first lesson at home is that she is unloved, then the first lesson she needs to learn at school is that there she *is* loved.

"And if a child's first lesson at home is that she *is* loved, then the first lesson she needs to learn at school is that there she is loved *also*.

"Most professional teachers are bad teachers. Not because they *are* bad teachers. But because we allow teachers to take their orders not from those who want the best *for* children, but who want the best *from* them.

"If we want our professional teachers to be the good teachers they could be, we must respect them not only with our lips, but also with our plaudits and our purse.

"And if we countenance bad teaching we cannot be surprised if our children are taught badly.

"The good teacher knows his best tool is not his mouth but his ears.

"In our search for ourselves, curiosity is the compass.

"Good teachers reverence that curiosity. It pushes the pupil in the direction the pupil needs to go. Because pupils are the best teachers, it will be likely also to lead the teacher whither the teacher needs to go.

"That we are not professional teachers does not mean we are not teachers. We are all, all of us, teachers all of the time.

"And teaching is the most important job we all, all of us, have to do.

"If we are good teachers and wise teachers we are also pupils all of the time. All of us look for example, and all of us are examples.

"Sometimes we are good examples, often bad. But that we are an example of bad does not mean we are not good teachers. If thereby we stop the infant from playing with the flames, the burns we suffered have served an infant well. We can wear the scars as badges of pride."

The prophet sat down on a large stone. He brought his legs up to a ledge further down that stone that he could balance comfortably.

"Knowledge is not learning," he said. "It can be a stepping stone to learning. It can also be an obstacle to it. To wisdom often it is a bar.

"We are awash with knowledge today. Everywhere there is a glut, a flood of knowledge. We're drowning in that knowledge.

"And wisdom? The wisdom available would barely fill an eggcup.

"We do not educate our children today, we apprentice them. We are leading them not to a knowledge of themselves but to be vassals for industry.

"We do not look at a child and see a chest bursting with love and potential. We see a cog to be honed down until it fits the machine.

"This is madness posturing as sanity.

"This is blasphemy posing as piety.

"This is the lie insisting, as the lie always does, it is the truth."

•••

"**AND** what of children?" asked an old and toothless woman, who held a goat on a leash at her side. Her face was swathed in a scarf of wool, but she seemed as impervious to the sun's heat as she was to the flies swished by the goat's tail towards her. Her frame was slight, but its strength surged through every sinew. Saskja ran about her. The toothless woman frowned after the little girl.

"Almustafa speaks so beautifully of children," the prophet sighed.

"We abuse our children," he continued.

"We start to abuse our children when we see them as the personification of our hope and not that of their own hope.

"It is one of the ten commandments that we should honour our father and our mother. I cannot help wondering how much kinder a place the world would be today if that injunction had read instead: 'Honour thy children'.

"Honour is begat by being honoured.

"If children are honoured by their parents, they will need no edict in later life commanding them to honour their parents. Such will happen as naturally as thawing snow creates waterfalls. Even without it, many children not honoured by their parents still honour them.

"To frame this natural inclination as a command is to demand of today it suppress tomorrow's needs in favour of yesterday's.

"Those of us who have been parents have been paid the highest compliment. We have been entrusted to tend the future until the future can tend itself. It is the most difficult and, with teaching, the most important job in the world.

"So often it is in parenting our children that we start the also difficult, also important task of parenting ourselves.

"Because we live in a world where madness postures as sanity, it is the job which is respected the least. For which less training is given than for any other.

"We think because we have been children this qualifies us to guide other children.

"We think because children have been reared since the beginning of time that the rearing of children is innate.

"We have distorted the innate so violently that nothing any longer can, with safety or accuracy, be called such.

"That the future should respect the past is self-evident. The future should even honour the past. If the past has tended it well, the future should indeed incorporate the past.

"But we, parents of Orphalese, we have abused the future.

"We have created an arsenal of time-bombs. Most of them are primed. And when we have not done this ourselves, we have allowed others to do so. Often in our names.

"We have allowed our children's heads to be filled with half-truths and quarter-truths and obfuscations. Yes, and lies. We have allowed learning to be replaced by propaganda. We have sold our souls, and theirs, for gewgaws and trinketry.

"Children of Orphalese, honour your mothers and your fathers when they do not command you to honour them, but when they suggest that you honour yourselves."

●●●

A portly and ruddy-faced man stood up in the crowd. He asked: "And is there no laughter in this scheme of things?"

"Yes," said the prophet. "Oh *God*, yes. We are looking to build ourselves a happier life. How could you have a happy life without laughter?

"Laughter is the oil on the bread. It is also the jam on the bread. Life is possible without laughter but it would be drab and boring and oppressive.

"Laughter is also very wholesome, wonderfully healthy – miraculous indeed in its powers to heal. But it can also be unwholesome and unhealthy.

"It depends," said the prophet, "whether we aim our laughter outside of us or in. Whether we use it as a signpost to help us to the truth, or as a blindfold to shield us from it.

"Comedy, if we are wise, is laughing today at our telling tomorrow of what will then be our calamity of yesterday.

"If we are brave enough, it can also be a shield

against the barbarian. Nothing is rendered more feeble than that seen to be risible. But that, too, is why we need to be cautious of our laughter.

"If we laugh because we recognise in ourselves the weakness we are laughing at in others, that is healthy; if in order to hide it from ourselves, that aggravates a sickness.

"If we laugh to earth ourselves, that is healthy; if to exalt ourselves, sick.

"If we laugh *in* pain that is healthy, *at* pain it is unhealthy and unwholesome.

"If the laugher emanates from love, it is a healthy laughter; if from hatred it is toxic.

"If we laugh to scorn the torturers, that is healthy; if we laugh that we may become a torturer, that is depraved.

"When the jester mocks us he helps us. When he mocks our neighbours he debases us. When he mocks us he denudes the barbarian; when he mocks our neighbours we *become* the barbarian."

•••

SHE was in her mid-thirties and heavily pregnant. Her soft grey eyes were radiant with fulfilment. Platinum hair sheened down her back, with the grace of swans dunking in the pond. There was a dimple of amused curiosity curling about her lip.

"Is there no allowance made," she asked, "for us to be human?" Arkona smiled. He chuckled. "Are you laughing at me?" the blonde woman asked. She was not sharing the joke.

"At *me*," Arkona replied. "No, no, not at you. At *me*. At how preposterous I am. That's one form my own humanness takes: my preposterousness.

"Frailty's name is not woman, it is human. It is so human it defines us. Rather than wag our fingers at the frailty of others we should rejoice in it.

"It makes life more interesting, more fun. It makes life life. We would otherwise be sharing this planet with nothing better for company than automatons.

"I am so human, *so* human. And I manifest my

humanness when I forget that. When I seek to be other than human. To be super-human, or extra-human. It is then I become preposterous. And then it is I am completely human.

"I have spoken before of the tornado within me – within us.

"Those who hear voices are, by so much of the world, dubbed 'insane'. I say this to you: Those who are truly insane are those who do not hear voices, or who hear the lone voice. We who are sane (though human) hear voices all the time, at least two voices the *entire* time: the voice of 'stay' and the voice of 'go'; those of 'safety' and 'adventure', of 'me' and 'us'.

"We can only obey the exhortations of one voice. We are always in conflict, therefore, with another one. Sometimes we obey wisely, sometimes foolishly.

"If we are to take the job seriously of loving ourselves we must learn to forgive ourselves. We walk fine lines – tightrope wires. Are we being fair if we admonish ourselves for falling?

"A certain amount of shame will stop us repeating the same mistake; too much will inhibit us from moving forward.

"We only obey wrongly if we know our actions will hurt another.

"So many of us today are in so much pain because we know we're obeying wrongly and can see no alternative. If there *is* no alternative, then we also need to forgive ourselves for obeying wrongly.

"God loves the sinner who repents because repenting is in God's own interest. God can most fully be experienced by those who love themselves. It is almost impossible to love yourself unless you can forgive yourself. Repentance is the first step to forgiving yourself.

"To forgive sins is not to forget them, nor is it to countenance them. It is to forbid them also from contaminating today.

"The mother who does not forgive herself for smacking a child will smack more children than she who can.

"It is hard to love the sinful. It is hard to love ourselves when we are sinful. As hard as it is easy to love the virtuous. Yet we are, all of us, both sinful and virtuous. The sister who refuses to see, or to acknowledge, the mote in her brother's eye – or in his character – does not love him. And when we do not accept the mote in our own eye, or character, we do not love ourselves.

"Never will we fully forgive others. Or ourselves. Nor can we fully love ourselves. Or others. Precisely because we *are* human. And being human means we can do nothing – nothing at all – perfectly. The accomplishment can never be in the done. There is no done. There is only the doing."

•••

AND a clown stood up, his eyes lively and of a lively green. Not the sad clown, he, but the clown happy to bestow his happiness. "Talk to us," the clown said, "of death."

"We use one word, 'death', but we use it for three distinct phenomena: the process of dying, the end of life, and the confiscation of life.

"Death is not the sadness. Dying can be. It is grieving which always is.

"We are all dying.

"It is so simple, that truth, so inescapable. And yet we seek to thrust it from us like the spoilt child who will not eat his broccoli.

"The end of life is not the enemy.

"The atom of creation contains within itself the seed of its own destruction. It has to. It is precisely that which makes it life.

"To resent death is to resent life. They cannot exist without each other. Indeed they define each other.

"We will never know the mystery of death.

Because if we could know it, it would no longer *be* death. Just as if we were ever to know God, whatever it was we then did know could not be God.

"There are few efforts more vain than to seek to penetrate the mystery of death. But in so vainly dissipating our resources, we find ourselves short of the energy we need to fight the real foe.

"The sadness of death is not in the event but, often, in the process preceding it and, always, in the process succeeding it.

"Nothing can prepare you for death.

"But everything can prepare you for dying.

"We are best ready for dying when we are living as fully as we can.

"In the process of dying we continue to teach. Maybe even especially during that process.

"Those who have been diagnosed terminally ill and who are berating Fate and cursing God have already succumbed. They are genuflecting at death's altar.

"Some of the terminally sick, though, demand of death it wait its turn. Some of these get so busy living they lack the time to die. These are the terminally healthy.

"The terminally healthy teach us nothing about death. Death is unteachable. But they do teach us much about living. The terminally healthy seek to heal rifts and not enlarge them; they hanker for peace and reconciliation, for forgiveness and to forgive. The terminally healthy understand love from an entirely new perspective – and with greater vigour than before they'd have believed possible.

"The terminally healthy have respect for the terminally ill.

"It is we, for the moment more hale, who debase the terminally ill. If we allow death to be the foe, we allow life to be confiscated during the dying process. If we allow death to be the foe, we allow that dignity and comfort be considered luxuries.

"If we allow death to be the foe, death is always a defeat.

"But it is a convenient defeat. It allows us to invest all our resources into one moment of defeat.

"If we allow death to be the foe, we dissipate our ability to mollify our own grief, or to tender the support craved by others who may be grieving. Because grief is not a moment, but a process. Those who are bereaved have no need of momentary solacers – their grief is so numbing at that time they will barely notice it. Their need is for those prepared to stay with them during a process – often several processes.

"Death is not the enemy. Often the enemy is the process of dying. The *confiscation* of life, however, that is always the enemy.

"We confiscate life when we promise plenty in paradise instead of sufficient on Earth.

"We confiscate life whenever we subjugate the potential of others to our own comfort, whenever we seek not our betterment but mine.

"We confiscate life when we tyrannise or terrify or bully. We confiscate life when we build systems to enslave others or when we will not pay to stop their pain. The hungry and homeless have life confiscated from them. So do the angry and the giddy and those wantonly under-educated.

"Premature death, synthetic death, that is the ultimate confiscation of life. Murder, assassination, genocide. Murder by want, assassination by lack of medicines, genocide by financial manipulation. Synthetic death is thus the ultimate crime.

"And of that ultimate crime, state-sanctioned murder is the most wicked of all. Because such bloodies all of our hands and stains all of our consciences.

"War is state-sanctioned murder. So is capital punishment.

"If the state kills in our name, then it is our name which is sullied. We are as guilty as the train-driver who ferried the Jews to Auschwitz or the gunsmith who fashions the murder weapon.

"Not one execution in the world's history has made the world a better place to live in, or a safer. No, not even those of Christ or Eichmann.

"If the state kills, the state condones murder.

"To condemn that which you condone is not paradox. It is Janus with one face masked."

•••

"SO, what is truth, then?" asked a ploughman, his brawny arms glowing ripples in the dappled light.

"Shhh!" replied the prophet. "You will find neither truth nor *the* truth in words. Shhh!" the prophet said again.

"You will find truth," said the prophet after a time of quiet, "basking in your soil. You will find it in the change from seed to wheat.

"You will find truth in your horses' ears as they prick to new and unexpected sounds. And, yes, in their dung which feeds the soil. Truth is in the sky and in the clouds, in the birds sparkling in the hedgerows. And you will find it in all these places.

"Look for truth – look honestly for truth – and you will find yourself surrounded by truth, and immersed by it.

"If you have it, it cannot leave you.

"If you do not have it, it will find you.

"For the truth not to find you, you have not to want it. For it not to find you, you have to thrust the truth away.

"The emperors and the sultans command us to thrust the truth from us. And tempt us with treasure that we do so. They insist that the truth is *not* the truth and keep talking so that the quiet cannot tell us otherwise.

"The emperors and the sultans do not want us to know the truth. Because a part of that truth is that they are not powerful at all. They have power only because we cede them power.

"And the treasure that they offer? It is to reward your arm for chopping down a tree by cutting off your hand.

"Citizens of Orphalese, you are teachers. You have the power to teach the world to teach and to teach the world to learn.

"When the world has learnt truth, there will be no more war because the citizens will no longer believe the generals.

"And when the world has learnt truth, there will be no more babies crying to a famished sleep because the citizens will no longer believe the bankers.

"And the journey will still be a trek through swamps of crocodiles and quicksand, but more of the world will recognise that trek to be a paradise indeed.

"And of that knowledge will spring a greater paradise, one where we heed the warnings about quicksand, and where we see crocodiles more as demanding room-mates than threats.

"And that knowledge, my friends, is knowledge worth its knowing."

●●●

HIS eyebrows seemed to be one. His beard-line was heavy. The hair beneath his knuckles was black. Dark brown eyes seemed to have embedded themselves deeper in his skull. But they shone with curiosity and burned with understanding. "Anger?" he asked.

Again Arkona chuckled. "No," he said quickly. "Again I am laughing at myself. Believe me, not at you.

"Anger!" the prophet said. "All my life I have wrestled with anger." He paused, just for a moment. "It is like wrestling with eels.

"It's possible to use anger wisely. But that is a skill I have never acquired.

"Anger is like emotional pain. Like pain it is a good indicator that there is something wrong. Like pain, too, there are many different types of it.

"But, unlike pain, it is deceptive. We think it is our children angering us when it is our overseer; we think it is the cashier angering us when it is the bank.

"That which threatens me angers me. A cat backed into a corner will become a tiger. The anger of others backs *us* into a corner. It is very threatening.

Which is one of the reasons anger is so infectious.

"That which wounds me angers me. Wounds my pride or my peace, my dignity, my security or my welfare. Also wounds my pride *and* my peace, dignity, security *and* welfare.

"That which wounds my propriety angers me, or my ethics.

"Blessed indeed is she who can restrict her anger to the act and not the actor. I strive to be so blessed, but am not.

"I find it impossible to look at the world today and not be angered.

"We have this beautiful, beautiful planet which we are annihilating.

"We have these beautiful, beautiful creatures on it which we are allowing to perish.

"We are teetering on the very edge of self-destruction. Because a handful of plutocrats cannot control their addiction to their acquisitiveness.

"We are eroding, or allowing to be eroded, the very values which separated the civilised from the barbaric.

"We are condoning the exploitation of children.

"Everywhere you turn you see truth turned on its head by sophisticated forms of word-games and self-justification. We are self-justifying ourselves to our own destruction.

"I don't know how not to get angry about such things.

"I find myself angry at the presidents and plutocrats and premiers who continue to endorse such policies, even to advocate them. ... I find it irksome that I am supposed to condone my own suicide.

"That is why I am not a prophet, but a man.

"When the Christ raged against the merchants in the temple, was that He at his most human? Or His most divine?

"It angers me too that I am told these crimes are being perpetrated in my name. I find it immoral that I am asked to endorse an immoral act. They are trying to make me an accessory.

"If I allow them to do that, tomorrow it will be me the victim of their crimes. Such history will whisper to you in the quiet.

"Those today victims of these crimes will not remain passive tomorrow. That too history teaches us.

"My rage, though, is misplaced. We won't pull ourselves back from the precipice by raging. The perpetrators are also victims. Finally Cain is a victim too.

"We know, citizens of Orphalese, that anger distorts. Which is one reason that the person who angers us bests us.

"The cunning use our anger as their weapon.

Angry we do not see clearly. We aim at the wrong targets. We do not act rationally.

"She who can suppress her anger will always win out over her who cannot.

"Anger needs a present target. It is frustrating to get angry with

institutions or corporations. There is nowhere that the anger can penetrate. We need to shrink the target, and to personalise it.

"That is the principal role of politicians today.

"Long since did politicians resign from forming policy. That is dictated to them by those selfsame institutions and corporations.

"Politicians are there so that we can be angry with them, and leave those institutions and corporations alone so that they can, unnoticed, continue to wreak their ecological, moral and human havoc.

"But politicians too can only personify the institutions, they cannot be ranted at or complained to.

"So we shout at those we can – and at those it is safest to. The weaker of our acquaintanceship. We abuse our friends, our partners, our children or our pets. They in turn abuse their friends, their pets. A man kicking a dog is in great pain.

"Some of us are so angry – and with nowhere to put that anger – that we start to commit crimes against the innocent person in the street.

"Some others of us seek succour for our anger in momentary uplifts: drink, perhaps, or sex or drugs or chocolate or exercise or work. Still we prefer to supply the kicker with soft-soled shoes rather than insist she stop the kicking. And then we wonder that we are bruised. And hurting.

"It is so simple: Hurt people hurt people.

"Anger begets anger.

"The wise who anger apologise promptly. The wise who are the butt of anger learn to absorb it. To absorb anger requires the same leap of faith as grasping a nettle. Likewise it can neutralise the pain.

"Not to anger is not human. But to not-anger is to wrench from the barbarian one of his most powerful tools.

"Maybe we can never succeed in not-angering, but we can strive towards it. And we can strive not to be angry with ourselves for being angry with others. The reward, here too, is not in the done but in the doing."

•••

UNDER an olive tree, surrounded by his wife and teenage children, sat a balding man, his moustache and sideboards like dandelion clocks of silver. His children squirmed when he spoke, and sought to feign they were not with him. "Tell us of hypocrisy," said the balding man.

"Amongst us mortals," said the prophet, "only those who have no mark do not fall short of it. Only if you aspire to nothing will you not fail.

"The innkeeper enriched by drunkenness and urging greater temperance is perforce a hypocrite. But he is also a good man. He is screaming in the dark for a mentor.

"In the world today only the starving or the cynical can live without some hypocrisy – those famished either of food or spirit.

"We all live in countries which perpetrate or countenance violations of human rights. All of us who have a profession, and most of us who have jobs, are gaining our income from an activity which involves a compromise in ethics.

"That is the reality of the world today.

"Go into the quiet. Ask in that quiet whether that has always been the case, whether that *needs* to be the case. Whether that is not part of the human condition; and whether a compromise in ethics does not remind us, not one of us can have either all the answers nor the whole answer. Not one of us indeed can have the whole question.

"Maybe the quiet will tell you all we can do about that reality is to recognise that that *is* what it is: reality.

"Which is not to condone our hypocrisy. It is to recognise the distinction between the peccadillo and the felony. Sometimes it seems harder to forgive ourselves our peccadilloes than our felonies.

"We enjoin others usually to enjoin ourselves.

"If we accept a degree of personal hypocrisy to be inevitable we will not allow our embarrassment – or our fear of being thus branded – to stop us from espousing those concepts we believe to be the truth.

"For the Press to pillory idealists as hypocrites is the harlot lambasting the unmarried mother for her promiscuity. For the politician to censure Utopians for their hypocrisy is the mamba accusing the mosquito of being venomous.

"Let us not confuse a degree of our own hypocrisy – the inevitability of that hypocrisy – with the hypocrisy of multi-national business or of government.

The woman taking a kitchen knife to her drunken and abusive husband is not committing the same crime as the mob lynching or the state guillotining.

"Personal hypocrisy is one of those frailties that come with being human. The wise acknowledge its presence in themselves, check themselves whenever they can, but do not allow it to deflect them from pursuing their truth.

"Official hypocrisy is not so sanguinely to be countenanced.

"It is not to be countenanced, a Press which demands its freedom but has no respect for that of others; or which rails against attacks on innocent people whilst it attacks innocent people.

"It is not to be countenanced companies which support children's charities in one country and exact their exploitation in another.

"Nor is it to be countenanced, the hypocrisy of a state which extols the sanctity of democracy yet overthrows a democratic state if it disagrees with the vote; nor which enjoins its citizens to settle their differences whilst it prepares for war; nor which demands its citizens obey its courts whilst it disobeys an international court.

"The difference between personal hypocrisy and official hypocrisy is that between the braggart and the blagger.

"The braggart in short order becomes his own victim.

"The blagger will use his sawn-off shotgun if anything comes between him and his goal.

"Go into the quiet. Let the quiet define for you which is braggart – and which armed robber."

●●●

"TRAGEDY," said a man in his sixties, "is an inevitable part of life. If we are wise, we can use tragedy to grow." He was wearing an open-necked shirt of green checks. His eyes were rheumy, and deep furrows trenched his cheeks.

"Tragedy *is* inevitable," said the prophet. "Which means we have no need to manufacture it. When the Buddha said, 'Life is suffering,' that (in my opinion) is what he meant. The process of living already and inevitably involves suffering. Such suffering needs no manmade additives.

"Tragedy *is* endemic to life. So is inequity.

"If tragedy is endemic, the noise-makers seem to argue, for man to manufacture more is merely propagating a law of Nature. If inequity is endemic, inequity is obviously God's will and its propagation is therefore to be encouraged.

"The common cold, apparently, is also endemic. Would not that same argument suggest we should therefore propagate the cold virus?

"What would you call the man carrying sand to the Sahara?

"Nature supplies enough tragedy, enough inequity. Humankind has no need to manufacture more.

"Often, as you say, tragedy can be used as a tool to help us grow. Only a widow can fully understand the pain of widowhood. Tragedy used wisely can ripen into empathy. But to use it thus is a skill," said the prophet.

"We seem to believe the imparting of that skill to be God's job. We seem to expect that we be *born* with it. Do we not, when we cede that responsibility to God, blaspheme against the divinity contained by *us*?

"One of the most encouraging things today is that so many *are* now starting to take that responsibility. Widows are not only talking to widows, they're also talking about the need to talk to widows, and about the need to talk. And about the need to care. Widows to widows, abused children to abused children, parents to parents – even, yes, abusive parents to abusive parents.

"Once two lost people have found the other they are no longer quite so lost. They may not know where they are, but they are no longer nowhere. Together already they are somewhere. On a path to somewhere else.

"More and more people are like you, citizens of Orphalese, wise like you. They are beginning to understand that it *is* by inviting others into Eden that we enter it. It is by distributing our wisdom that it grows.

"More and more people understand that if the end of wisdom is not to make the world a happier place whatever is being called wisdom is not wisdom. It cannot be wisdom."

•••

THERE was a short, squat woman with curly grey hair and brown and canny eyes. A shawl of light blue silk lazed about her shoulders. "Talk to us of politics," she said.

"To put politicians in charge of a country," the prophet said, "is to put an alcoholic in charge of a bar.

"People who aspire to power are the last people who should be allowed it. Go into the quiet. Let history whisper to you its lessons.

"It is not as simple as that power corrupts – although it can do. Nor that absolute power corrupts absolutely – although it has to. It is that those who hanker for power are already corrupted.

"It is not only power itself but the desire for power which is toxic. The greater the desire for the greater the power the more venomous the toxin.

"We embrace a system of government where it is not the cream that rises to the top but the milk which is the most curdled.

"She who would have power over another, even in that desire, compromises herself.

"Even in his ambition the would-be general is already slaughtering his troops.

"The president is the human Pinocchio hankering to be made of wood again.

"Few are there – maybe four or five legislators in a century – of such inner resilience to want power for what they can cede, rather than what they can grab.

"It is in the hands only of these very few that power is safe.

"Power should be given only to those who shrink from it, as wax shrinks from the flame. It should be given only to those who would enjoin us to find the power within ourselves. And to those who do not seek solutions in noise, but questions in quiet.

"Power should only be given to those whose Cabinet also contains their critics, and whose inner circle also contains their lampoonists.

"It should only be given to those for whom humanity is the end and not the means.

"It should only be given to those who know power to be an illusion, but who are fully conscious of the enormous, and very real, peril contained within that illusion.

"Power should be given only to those who laugh."

•••

THEN spoke a father, maybe thirty, of three small children. His beard was trimmed and his torso lanky. "What of business?" he asked.

"If business is exchange and exchange is traffic, then," Arkona said, "it is good. If it is only legal theft," said the prophet, "then it is bad.

"If the thief steals from you, it's condemned as being criminal; if industry steals from you, it's countenanced as being the way of the world. That is a parlour game. But it is one with parlous consequences.

"If we exchange reasonable effort for reasonable return, it is good. If the effort expended is to render the return unreasonable, it is theft. Thus it is banks steal far more often than they are robbed.

"Theft also endorses theft. When a profiteer demands punishment for the man who picked his pocket, that is the rapist demanding vengeance for the pinching of his bottom.

"Business is no longer about exchange. It has become about toeing a hazy line of licitness defined by an executive which has been bribed by business.

"I'm getting angry. Sorry.

"When you steal from a worker also her ability to negotiate, that is a double theft. You steal cash from her, certainly, and confiscate life from her children. But you also steal her dignity – and yours. It is the theft of her birthright and your integrity. Theft always damages the thief more than the thieved. This double-theft damages the thief doubly.

"If you create an economic climate where the choice for the worker is between working for subsistence wages or starving, that is protection racketeering on a gigantic scale. Made worse because, in selling those workers into slavery, you also place yourself in bondage.

"And again you're getting angry," Saskja told him impishly.

"I am. You're right," he admitted. "Children are not always right. Nor are they always truthful. But there is always truth in a child. Even a child's lies hold truth," Arkona said.

"Business today," he continued, anger still teetering around the fringe of his voice, "is super-theft.

"Super-thieves steal from the poor and insist it is thus that the world's wealth is created.

"To create more wealth, the thieves argue, kings have to pass laws exempting the now-wealthy from obeying the law.

"So the kings pass laws to allow the already rich further to plunder the already desperately poor.

"And we wonder that by so many the law is held not to be something which protects them, but something which yokes them and shackles them and disempowers them. They see the law (often erroneously but not always) not as something which liberates them but something which terrorises them.

"When we bend the law to accommodate a vested interest we ourselves commit a massive crime.

"Such crimes cannot be perpetrated without the most enormous damage to the soul.

"Finally, to the world's soul.

"To the soul of those perpetrating such crime the damage is obvious.

"Even the souls of the victims are damaged. Nothing warps the soul more quickly than being denied the chance to nurture your children.

"If you live in a coal-mine you get coated in coal-dust. It takes remarkable energy to keep washing away that dust, to keep reminding yourself it is not a natural condition to be streaked with dust.

"It is a tribute to you, people of Orphalese, that so many of you have souls as clean as they are. But you are not alone, people of Orphalese. Not any more. Everywhere you go there are cadres of clean coal-miners. Strong enough to defy the taunts of those so sooted they can no longer see.

"Strong enough too to enjoy that irony that, if the taunters are to survive, they will need the unsooted eyes of the clean.

"Business is not business today but economic genocide.

"It is not industry but a system of control and terror. Eventually it is suicide.

"It is Narcissus demanding he is Zeus."

•••

"AND love?" asked a man in his fifties, his crewcut hair balding as if he had been tonsured, his right ear ringed. Soft blue eyes danced nervously above a gently aquiline nose.

"Love is God," said the prophet. "And God is love. God is truth. And truth is God. Love is therefore truth. And usually truth is love, but not always. And that is so because God, although It is resolution, is even more the riddle.

"Love is an agglomeration of most of the most important emotions that we have and yet we have only one word for it. We have only one word because, finally, it is one.

"We love our lovers. We love our parents, our children, our friends, our pets. Those of us who are blessed love our neighbours. A few who are doubly blessed love God.

"We love life and we love the world. We love a good meal, we love a special bottle of wine. We love freshly fallen snow and the call of Spring's first cuckoo; love this sculpture and that concerto; our house and our new car; the smell of newly mown grass and the feel of clean sheets; a happy ending and a roaring fire. We love birthdays and to cry at weddings.

"And all these *are* love. Let there be no mistake about that. Yet they are as different from each other as the cheetah is from the tortoise.

"Love is, of course, itself. And as itself it is both God and a part of God, and thus defies description or constraint. But love is not only Zeus. It is Eros too. Venus, Narcissus, Psyche and the Muses. There is love even in Mars.

"War is, of course, an abnegation of love. But there is love within a war.

"The soldier falling on a grenade to save his colleagues is performing an act of love; the private who carries his wounded sergeant back to the field hospital is loving a man back to life.

"Love is also a generic term for passion, adoration, worship, veneration, respect, reverence, lust, attraction, esteem, romance, concern, care, altruism, philanthropy, devotion, charity, selflessness, great fondness and great liking. And it is right that it means all these things, because it contains them all.

"It is also thought of as a synonym, though it is the antonym, for obsession, infatuation, sentimentality and addiction.

"It is rarely the lyrics of popular songs speak wisely. But, as the words of one have it, love does make the world go round. Love also gives point to the world going round.

"We have to love. Humankind has to love. Which is both its glory and its tragedy.

"It is our glory when we love wisely.

"But we *have* to love. If we do not love wisely, there is no other option but to love unwisely.

"If we do not love ourselves, and thus God, we love Mammon. If we do not love the sunset we love prestige. If we do not love the dew frosted on the fern we love sycophancy. If we do not love our children we love gold. If we do not love to laugh we love to make others cry.

"It is not possible to love wisely unless you love yourself. To love yourself it is a requirement that you respect yourself.

"If you respect yourself you do not allow maharajahs to wrest what should be your power from you nor treat you with anything other than respect.

"Which is one of the reasons the world's maharajahs feel threatened when we do respect ourselves and when we enjoin others also to respect *them*selves. And why the maharajah's jesters feel enjoined to mock us when we do.

"There is a pandemic abroad, far more dangerous than smallpox, as planet-threatening as anthrax.

"It is the pandemic of self-hatred.

"This pandemic of self-hatred is anthrax of the soul.

"More devastating yet than anthrax because it robs us, as well as of life, of dignity and humanity and honour.

"The world is in the apocalyptic state it is not because we do not love our neighbours as ourselves, but because we do: We *hate* our neighbours as ourselves.

"Many – perhaps most – of us have been so badly bruised, usually in childhood, that, even knowing the perils involved in not loving ourselves, we *cannot.* The intellect can never master the emotions. It can instigate a process, though, which *can* alter those emotions.

"We can, all of us, respect ourselves, for instance.

"And respect can lead to love.

"We can respect ourselves initially by respecting the commitment we have made to respecting ourselves. Even if that respect is sired only by respecting the honesty we have unearthed to acknowledge we do not yet do so.

"From that respect love can be born. Quite as real a love as any other. And once love has entered your life, you will no longer fear the quiet nor wish to ignore its ministrations.

"There is a paradise on this Earth just waiting for the seeding.

"All we need do to seed it is to allow love to do

its job, and let it – and not Mammon or distrust or insecurity or hatred – make the world go round.

"Citizens of Orphalese, you are wise. You know it is not an indulgence that we love ourselves. To the contrary. Often it is the hardest thing to do in life. But it is the planet's requirement if it is to continue to support human life. It is the final obligation we have both to our children and to the whole of humankind.

"You know, citizens of Orphalese, not to do the work necessary to love ourselves is to bury a dagger in humanity and to violate the sacred spirit, our own sacred spirit. It is to procure our own destruction and our own damnation.

"Go into your quiet.

"Let your quiet whisper to you its confirmation of that.

"Or not.

"Start enjoining the neighbours now you are able truly to love also to go into their quiet.

"They will love you for it. Because they too will now be able to.

"They will have started loving themselves."

•••

"I'M sorry," said the ear-ringed man. "I was talking more of secular love. The falling-in-love sort of love."

"The love which is romance?" asked the prophet.

"Quite," said the ear-ringed man.

"Romance also means fiction," said the prophet. "Make sure your love is not fiction.

"It is one," said Arkona: "the love of God, the love of truth, the love of another person. It all starts with love of yourself.

"And if you do love yourself you will be able to be in love with another. And all the world's hatred will not be able to stop you from being in love with another. And should that other stop loving you that will not stop you loving yourself.

"If you love yourself you will *not* fall in love. You will march into love, head erect, eyes fully open.

"If you love yourself you will understand the elements of any relationship: the 'me', the 'you' and the 'us', as you will understand that all those elements need venerating too, and for themselves as much as for their being components.

"If you love yourself you will recognise yourself to be exactly fifty per cent of any relationship you have, and will adjust any unequal relationship until it becomes so.

"If you love yourself you will be making love with the truth.

"And will therefore oust the lie from your bed, and let the lie return to its seduction of those viziers and princes who seek to enslave you.

"True love loves true lovers and true lovers love true love.

"You do not have to know there is a God for you to have one.

"The lover, whether or not she knows there is a God, knows God."

●●●

A young woman let go of her lover's hand. Jet hair sheened down her olive back. She wore a sarong of lime and an armful of delicate bangles which tinkled each frequent time her hand veiled her tinkling grin.

"Sex?" she asked and blushed. "What of sex?"

"What a disservice those who should know better have done to sex," said the prophet. "Sex is not humankind's debasement but its triumph. It is not the nadir of God's creativity but its zenith.

"God's greatest miracles are not manifested in the phenomenal, but in the mundane. To walk on water is a conjuring trick. To turn water into wine is less of a miracle than turning water into sweat. We wonder at the extraordinary, and will not see the wonder in the ordinary.

"To create life, to create *a* life, that is a miracle indeed.

"We are so misguided in our reverence – and our revelry. We want our messiahs to be circus performers. We seek spectacle not sight.

"Messiahs arrive not to awe you with miracles

around you, but to awaken you to the miracle which is you and to the miracle which is within you – and to that messiah too within you.

"The noise deafens us to the miracles which bombard us. We are like jackdaws, attracted by tinsel and not by substance. The miracle is not the car but the oil, not the radio but the radio-wave, not the jet but the fly.

"Sex is another miracle.

"The very clumsiness of sex is seized with the most perfect grace, into its very carnality is engraved its most sublime spirituality. Those are already two of its miracles.

"When we give ourselves sexually, it is in all senses that we expose ourselves. As such it is not only life-giving, but a metaphor for it. Self-exposure is a requirement of creation.

"In all humankind's aspiration to know God, or to emulate God, or to be God, at no time is it closer than when involved in sex.

"It is the ultimate act of giving and receipt, and where both not only feed off each other but are also one and the same. This too is a miracle. In this too it brings humankind closer to God.

"Sex is an act of consummate trust.

"We are never more easily wounded than when we are unarmoured. We are never more unarmoured than when involved with sex. If we abuse that trust, we abuse not only our lover but also creation and creativity and the spirit of both.

"Even if we are having sex only with our bodies. Even if the union is merely physical.

"I have heard priests claim that venereal disease is God's punishment for an over-indulgence in immoral sex. Does not that claim have about it the same spiritual profundity as that flu is God's punishment for an over-indulgence in immoral breathing?

"If it is an act of tenderness and of mutual giving there is nothing immoral about sex that is only physical. It lacks an important dimension and may therefore be less satisfying, but it is not immoral.

"To say of sex that it should be exclusive to married couples is to say that eating should be restricted to the well-fed.

"To claim that one act of sex is acceptable and another perverse or abhorrent is to seek to constrain a miracle.

"Monogamy is no more a requirement of a healthy sexual life than monotheism is a requirement of a healthy spiritual life. For many it is. Democracy, if it means anything, however, means the defence of the few.

"Provided they are consensual and between adults, provided that they are undertaken in the interests of giving and receiving pleasure, there are no abhorrent sexual practises. Only practises which an individual may find abhorrent. No one has the right, or the ability, on behalf of other people to define either. To be an arbiter of the propriety of sexual practises is to choose the world's menu.

"Clearly, though – and equally –, it is not just the act of sex which has to be consensual, but the acts.

"The exchange of a gift of kindness can never be immoral.

"Consensual sex between adults is never immoral. It is always a miracle.

"One joy which contains a fistful of miracles. This is no gewgaw of an orb or sceptre. This is a treasure indeed.

"The miracle of sex is that it is not just the miracle of life.

"Sex is the bliss of Heaven adapted for human consumption.

"It is God's thank you for putting up with life."

●●●

"WHO defines morality, then?" asked a woman of advancing years. Her hair was of a red too fiery to be natural. Her face had seen much adversity and yet the eyes had triumphed by smiling through it. The hands which stroked her chin were chiselled by pain and gnarled by labour. Yet they could still chuck a baby's cheek with the lightness of a moth.

"In the same way as, for God to be God, God must be *your* God," said the prophet, "so for morality to be morality it must be yours. *You* define morality.

"Go into the quiet. Let the quiet define morality for you.

"The noise creates only an ersatz morality.

"An ersatz morality frowns on two lovers enjoying sex, but condones a lack of health care for the elderly.

"It disapproves of two homosexuals holding hands in public, but allows food to be destroyed rather than distributed to the starving.

"Is that double-think? Is that a distortion of morality? Would your quiet countenance it? Or describe it as a distortion?

"My quiet tells me *my* morality is only consideration. And consideration is kindness. And kindness is understanding.

"Let your quiet tell you.

"If morality is not a stepping-stone to empathy is the morality a real one?"

●●●

AND a warrior who was visiting Orphalese stood up. His face was disfigured by a hundred scars, the eyes' lustre had been slain in some distant battle. And yet within this warrior too there was thirst for understanding.

"Tell us, then, of war," the warrior said. There was no challenge in his tone, but a childlike curiosity at variance with his wizened face.

"We should dress your wounds," the prophet told him. "We should swaddle you in love. The scars that disfigure your body you have a thousandfold within. Those prepared to do so can feel those wounds.

"When soldiers bleed they do our bleeding for us. And when their widows and their orphans weep they do our weeping for us. But soldiers and widows alike weep also for the lie which felled the fallen.

"War is not inevitable. Wars make war inevitable. Each war of the gore-steeped twentieth century had its roots in earlier wars. Kings do not protect their subjects by making war. You do not protect tomorrow by making enemies today. Or by aggravating feuds today.

"In the whole history of the world there have only ever been two conflicts: that between David and Goliath, and that between equals.

"When Goliath dons armour, he dons too the dignity and ethics of the playground bully. He seeks to steal lunch-money so that he can emblazon his breastplate with gold. Meantime the robbed go hungry.

"When the scrap is between two equals it is a bare-knuckle brawl where both keep slugging until the result is academic. Both are damaged and bloody and toothless.

"It is not that kings or generals *want* to desensitise their soldiers, or dehumanise them, it is that they *have* to. Soldiers have to become two-legged guard-dogs, as conscience-bereft as guard-dogs, as savage, as loyal to their master.

"And then the kings and generals throw up appalled hands when their troops act appallingly.

"The humanness of human beings, however," the prophet continued, "is remarkably resilient. So is their humanity. It is almost impossible completely to dehumanise a human being. Only rarely do even prisons succeed in that task; only rarely do even the most abusive parents.

"It is a testament to the humanness and humanity of humankind, when the soldier's bloody battle-dress is replaced by civilian clothes, how quickly and readily and completely most soldiers re-adopt the mores of a less bloody, less goose-stepped society.

"Do the kings help with this transition? Do the generals? Do we?

"We place ribbons on the soldier's breast to veil the thousand lesions of his heart. The generals award their troops such trinketry and the king pins the gewgaws on and we applaud, and we all consider our responsibility discharged.

"We repay selflessness by abandoning those who bled and wept on our behalf, the wounded and the widowed. We offer them rags for their wounds, and an ensign-embossed handkerchief for their tears. And forget them.

"You do not see the losing generals begging on street corners, but you do see veterans, who have lost limbs or wits. And you see those on whose behalf they bled and wept, sneering at those veterans and wishing they did not clutter up the pavement.

"War is not inevitable. Kings make war inevitable. Kings are never more necessary than in war. Kings want war to secure their own position.

"War is inevitable because kings have to have enemies.

"Kings have to have enemies because kings have to have armies. Kings tell their subjects such armies are there to protect those subjects from attack. More are they there to prevent those subjects from attacking.

"Kings have enemies abroad to still discontent

at home.

"War is not inevitable. Armies make war inevitable. If there is an army there will be a war. You do not buy a race-horse to pull a carriage."

The prophet paused for a while, and tried to let some in the assembly find their quiet.

"No nation ever won a war," the prophet said.

"A few generals have won *from* a war, but never a nation.

"History tells us differently because kings and generals must have their adulation. They have to have their triumphs. Less to validate their conquests than themselves.

"What was 'great' about Alexander? He was a drunk who was cruel to the point of psychosis. No general of Rome was awarded a triumph unless he had killed at least five thousand human beings. Yet we talk deferentially of Roman 'civilisation'. Julius Caesar slaughtered more than one hundred thousand people: the epitaph not of a hero, but a genocide. Yet still we remember him in our calendar.

"And we wonder there is violence on our streets?

"History is not about glorious battles and heroic kings. History is about men dying in misery and agony and degradation so that other men may become kings.

"In distorting history, we adulate not only our

own executioner but the hangmen of our children. If we allow historians to venerate mass murderers we cannot be surprised if our own children too are butchered.

"Progress, if it means anything, means only towards civilisation. Civilisation, if it means anything, must include peace. A civilised war is as possible as a hot snowball.

"To wage war in the name of peace is to create a desert in the name of irrigation.

"The only thing fostered by war is more war.

"Listen to the quiet. The quiet will tell you: the only way to stop war is to stop warring. You only stop warring by making a commitment to stop warring. You do not do so by making more weapons. That is to try and douse the flames with paraffin.

"Listen to the quiet. The quiet will tell you: At the end of any war, even the victor is a loser. And in the ashes of the rubble is germinated the seed of the next war.

"This, so the quiet will tell you, is not a sensible way of settling differences or of conducting world affairs.

"This is madness posturing as sanity."

•••

"VALIDATION," said a short, round-faced man. He wore glasses as round as his face. He was trying to mask his baldness by growing the remaining strands to beyond their normal length. These strands were constantly fluttering in the breeze. The man's hands were thus often at his head resetting them. "You talked about the need for validation."

"Yes," said Arkona, "it is a need," he said.

"Few indeed are there of us strong enough to need their validation only from within. And many of those are not the self-sufficient but the demented or the despotic.

"One of the reasons money has become the god to so many that it has is that it is thought a short cut – or a sure cut – to validation.

"The noise-makers try to tell us today our worth is measured by our wealth.

"So many of the wealthy are so unhappy because they still believe the myth. And wealth has *not* brought them validation. Therefore there must be something wrong with them. And they cannot understand what.

"If wealth is bought by the misery of others you will never find validation. Your own quiet will not allow you that validation. Because greed is hatred. And hatred's first victim is always its harbinger.

"It is another healthy trend today, the lack of respect held for the super-wealthy – the lack of validation ceded them.

"This despite the fact that it is the super-wealthy who control almost all the media and who use most of these vast resources to infect humanity with their distortions.

"When we cease to cede validation to these plutocrats we do start to change the world.

"Few of these super-rich mind being unpopular. Indeed they wreak a distorted inner validation from it. Let their *external* validation be forfeit, however, and they would believe themselves invalid. And that is to return them to the nightmare whence they thought their wealth had led them.

"We can start bestowing validation on those who have none, and who, if the world is to survive, need it: those maimed either physically or mentally, emotionally or spiritually.

"Bestowing such validation is no simple task.

"But the damaged will not be repaired by being sneered better or hated better. They will not be tortured into being whole, or dragooned into it. Logic will not complete them, or confinement, starvation or sarcasm.

Enjoinment, threat, cajoling, sulking or violence. There is only one tool which has a chance. You know the name of that tool as well as I do.

"They may not even be loved into being better. But, if they are to find love for themselves, that is the *only* tool that stands a chance.

"If we love them enough some *will* find love for themselves. And those that start to love themselves will love others in order that they might love *them*selves.

"This love is not the mush of the plutocrats' sentimental movies, this love is hard and mature and very unsentimental. It allows for a host of disappointments and betrayals and relapses.

"We do not expect a man pulverised by a juggernaut to be given an aspirin and be evicted from the hospital.

"So many of the maimed have been pulverised by an entire fleet of juggernauts. Over and over again."

"Angry, angry, angry," said Saskja, playing around the prophet's feet.

"You're right," sighed Arkona. "I find it hard. It angers me. Even in the quiet it angers me.

"I find it hard – so hard – to look upon the potential of this planet and see it so dissipated, so abused, so under-developed. The maimed have so much to give. Why do we not help them to give us? We are shooing Santa Claus off the roof.

"An ogre lusts after a golden chariot. In order to get it, he kills an entire civilisation. Are the ogre's actions honourable actions?

"Go into the quiet. Your quiet. Not mine. Hear your quiet. Heed it.

"Let the quiet strip away all the packaging and the presentation. Let the quiet expose the goods for what they truly are. Do not let me tell you. Or them tell you. Let your quiet tell you.

"Let your quiet dictate to you to whom you would give your validation.

"It is a precious treasure. Bestow it wisely.

"Your very future indeed depends on your bestowing it wisely. *Your* future and the *lives* of your grandchildren.

"The future of the *planet* depends on your bestowing it wisely."

•••

"TALK to me of freedom," said the housewife breasting forty, whose black hair was brought back into a severe bun and the arch of whose eyebrows seemed to mimic the Cupid's bow of her mouth.

"In my youth," the prophet remembered, "I was wont to think that freedom could not be relative. Either you were free or you weren't.

"If, by a hair's breadth, the bars of the cage were wide enough for the bird to escape then the bird was free. If too narrow by a hair's breadth, then it wasn't. There is no such thing, I used to think, as almost free or not quite free. An open prison is still a prison.

"It is only in the quiet that I am completely free. It was in the quiet I discovered that truth. And with it the further truth that, of course, freedom *is* relative.

"I am imprisoned within a body. And for all that that body is a miracle, and its workings are a miracle, it still needs to breathe; it needs to ingest food, to extract from that food its energy, to expel the residue. That body needs to be protected against the weather and against the sharpness of pebbles and of twigs. It needs cleansing and rest.

"That body cannot fly or breathe underwater. It comprises skin which can be cut and bones which can break. It is liable to attack from a billion invisible foes. It is vulnerable, pregnable – and mortal.

"No matter how important I am, or think I am, no matter the wealth I have acquired, nor how, no matter how admirable or contemptuous, I will die.

"To feed my body and to clothe it, to provide safe shelter for my rest and those who depend on me I need to work.

"We are not free, people of Orphalese. We cannot be free.

"But there are those less free than others.

"Being vassals we do not need to become slaves.

"Blind allegiance, for instance, we owe to nothing and to no one. To continue in a bitter or unfulfilling relationship because society tells you such union *should* last is to enslave yourself. To continue visiting a family which belittles you because society tells you the family is good, that too is to enslave yourself.

"To fall into such debt that you are faced with the choice of penury or continuing in the employ of a bully is to enslave yourself.

"To salute the flag of a country which abuses

you is both to countenance that abuse and condone it. Does the gypsy salute the swastika?

"In the quiet there is freedom. In the quiet the spirit becomes a sprite. It can travel anywhere. It is not restricted by its own frame or form. It is a realm, the quiet, where the physical and metaphysical and abstract are all the same and all interchangeable. The only bondage is that to breathing, and to a knowledge that you cannot stay in the quiet always.

"It is also a realm which, if visited often enough, will free you from the fear of death. It will help you to your own realisation that death is not a curse but a blessing, not a manacle but a release.

"If that realm is visited more often yet, it will free you from fear of derision or censure.

"A few, frequent visitors, have freed themselves from the need for security or comfort. They are truly blessed.

"In the noise, we may be able to do little about our bondage. But we are free enough to know when we are bonded. And we are free to hear with incredulity the claims of those who jail us that they are freeing us.

"In the noise the truth may be inaudible. The lie, though, always betrays itself.

"Certainly you are free, too, to believe the lie.

"But why would you want to? Would that not be painting the 'Mona Lisa', then handing a scalpel to a picture-slasher?

"The noise-makers contend that you can only broaden your own bars by narrowing those of others.

"My quiet tells me this: Freedom paid for by the captivity of others is the freedom of a budgerigar who pays for the prising open of his cage by breaking his wings and his legs.

"Better by far to be the uncaged canary than the caged eagle. But better to be the caged canary than the eagle who cages the canary."

•••

A short woman stood up next. She was middle-aged, her hair now of more grey than the brown she'd been born with. The squirrelness of her face was exaggerated when she seemed to nibble at her words. "Talk to us," she said, "of crime and punishment."

"In the noise justice is a lie. In the noise we have handed justice over to the law. And the law has been handed over to lawyers.

"And sometimes the law is an ass. And sometimes lawyers make an ass of the law.

"An indication of the law's inadequacy is that it expects a line to be drawn on one side of which is innocence and on the other guilt. The law is not such an ass that it does not realise that such is, of course, absurd. But it makes life easier. It allows lawyers to question witnesses and not us our own consciences.

"It's a pragmatic position. It just isn't justice.

"The law is supposed to provide us with guide-lines to help resolve complex ethical dilemmas. It has been reduced by lawyers – as, whatever the rectitude of the lawyers, it had to be – to a rather unsophisticated game of chess.

"Do you really want your ethics decided on the result of a chess game? Are we really prepared to gamble with the lives of our fellow-creatures on the chess-playing skills of their advocates?

"How many judges," the prophet asked, "how many juries look into the quiet?

"When we condemn others it is ourselves that we condemn.

"The mob bays for blood not because of the hurt occasioned by a particular crime, however heinous that crime. That crime, the pain occasioned the individual by that crime, merely provides focus for the thousand separate pains from which each one in the mob is still hurting. It provides rage with an acceptable reason for its presence.

"Those in pain as a consequence of crime – the direct victims and the indirect ones – want their pain to stop. And if it cannot stop then to ease. They want their pain to be taken as a matter of some importance.

"If, by some quirk of fate, the leg cannot be set, then at least the victim welcomes some comfort. And some succour. They like to see some concern shown.

"The way to treat a broken leg is not to break someone else's.

"The only thing which prison teaches the bully is how to bully more ruthlessly. Prison is state-sanctioned bullying. The bully behind bars learns only to develop bigger muscles, and to hide his bullying behind authority. You do not learn temperance from a glutton.

"It is the human sacrifice to appease wrathful gods.

"Our concentration is misdirected. It is all on the sinner and not on the sinned against.

"In all but a handful of cases, sinning starts with being sinned against. If the sinned against were given some kind of guidance how to comfort themselves, how to receive solace, how much less would they want to sin against others.

"How much less sin would there be in the world.

"Citizens of Orphalese, it is so simple – it is *always* so simple: Hurt people hurt people.

"We are, all of us, hurt people; and we all, all of us, hurt people.

"Even those of us who do not mean to hurt people hurt people. Even those of us who think we have not.

"Hurting is sinning.

"There are maybe those of you, people of Orphalese, who think you have been sinned against but that you do not sin. I urge you – please – to go into the quiet.

"I think you will discover there that one of the penalties of life is that you cannot not sin. Even if our sinning is only by omission.

"We sin each time we allow an affront to dignity, each time we do not expose the lie, each time we falter before the bully, each time we ignore the scream or allow ourselves to be blinkered. We sin each time we see an act of cruelty go unchecked.

"Society is rarely surrendered the decision between right and wrong. If we are wise, it is our heart which determines what is moral; what is legal is determined by the state's brain. That brain determines what is permitted and what is not. And yet the state seeks to punish, not in its own name, but in that of society as a whole. It does not claim merely legality for itself, but morality.

"And it is precisely at that point that the law has to become an ass. It has assumed the grandiosity of the moral buffoon.

"The state decides that the man giving his terminally ill wife an overdose is a criminal, yet the hospital refusing treatment to that woman for lack of funds is behaving not only legally but morally. It sues journalists for withholding information and its own employees for leaking it, and in both cases claims also morality for itself.

"The mockery of the law will continue until a way is found of not rewarding sinning – all sinning, not just what the state in its arrogance and crassness designates sinning – and which does reward, also in material terms, not sinning.

"We have to stop penalising those whose work is of benefit to others: the nurses, the teachers, the parents. And have to stop rewarding those whose work is harmful: the gunsmiths, the legalised drug pushers, the fast-food restaurateurs – those lawyers whose interests are exclusively chess-based or cheque-based.

"Citizens of Orphalese, in all the noise who talks any longer of creating a better world?

"The world's mantra has become 'Life *is* unfair', as if such excused all injustice. Weeds grow. Does that stop us from pulling them from our flower-beds?

"The man who stops fighting for justice is he who has concreted over the flower-beds.

"In the noise, soon all the flower-beds will have been concreted over.

"Is this not madness? Is it posturing as sanity?"

•••

A tailor there was, not yet thirty, of cropped brown hair and thick and bushy eyebrows. His eyes were of the brown of chestnuts and stayed fixed on an invisible star beyond the cypress tree breaking the horizon of the hill's brow. "Talk to us, prophet, of Press freedom and freedom of speech. Of freedom of thought and freedom of expression."

"Shhh!" the prophet said again. "Listen to the still and you will find all such freedoms," said the prophet.

"What a beautiful thing is the Press. How express and admirable. It is a teacher, a friend, a *confidant*, a gossip. But because it is so beautiful, or could be so beautiful, we cede it enormous power. We allow it to form our opinions, because mostly it is from there that we extract the information upon which we base our decisions.

"Presently we are rewarded by the Press for this surrender by receiving in exchange a volatile cocktail of condescension and contempt."

"Angry, angry, angry," said Saskja again, again running through the prophet's feet. Arkona tried to smile at her, but his dimples held a glance of glower in them.

"The media today," Arkona said, "do not disseminate news but opinion. That is not information but propaganda.

"It is a legitimate use of Press freedom to express opinion, but not when such is feigning to be news. Nor when the opinion neglects the mention of certain facts uncomfortable to that opinion.

"Freedom," said the prophet, "if the commitment to it is complete, means self-constraint.

"Freedom of the Press is an awesome responsibility – both for those who write in the Press and for those of us who read.

"It is to publish those things which government wants secret but which the world has a right to know.

"The responsibility is to lay waste to prejudice and bias and, objectively, to lay the facts before us. And then for us objectively to read them. It is for both writer and reader to acknowledge – over and over again – that objectivity is an unattainable goal, and that the facts presented can – at their very best – only be those known to date.

"It is the responsibility to own that often news-that-is-reported is different from that which it would have been if unreported. And that knowledge that this news will be reported may well change the dynamic of the action before even the action is perpetrated. Sometimes before it is even considered. The media *create* news by their presence. And create news by their obsessions.

"The Press uses freedom when it exposes duplicity, and abuses it when it seeks to bury the important beneath the trivial.

"True freedom of the Press requires that you go into the quiet and ask that quiet to separate what is from what we would want it to be.

"It is to recognise that the value of news is not in the speed with which it is gathered but in the accuracy with which it is disseminated.

"It is to recognise that a franchised people has the right to expect that its sources of information take their receipt of that information seriously.

"It is to recognise that it is not only their words but their methods which are communicated throughout society.

"The invasion of privacy can only be justified when it *is* justified. Titillation does not justify it.

"When the Press exceeds its authority it countenances those excesses of the Executive or the Police. Because it makes it so easy for both of them to divert attacks. When the Press exceeds its authority it abuses its freedom and ours.

"When freedom is abused it is threatened.

"And those that abuse most the freedom of the Press are those most vociferous in the insistence of its sanctity. Is this not like the huntsman demanding protection for the fox?

"The world is not a better place, not a place of more compassion or freedom, for door-stepping the parents of a recent murder victim.

"It is in our name that these offences are perpetrated. Do we, the readers, really want the barons to debase us thus? Us, the readers; us, those who work for the barons; us, those innocents hounded by them?

"The Press will have regard for its own freedom and ours when we accept responsibility for their offences. When we stop buying newspapers that debase us all.

"You have no need to visit an abuser. That is *your* freedom.

"If the choice for a newspaper is between responsibility and bankruptcy, usually it will opt for responsibility.

"Just as your God can only be yours, no one else's truth can be your truth. Only the quiet can tell you what your truth is.

"Go into the quiet, and hear the opinions not of vested interest but of your own angels.

"And that, my friends of Orphalese, would be sanity portrayed as lunacy."

●●●

"**YOU** talked earlier of miracles," said a young woman with oval glasses and fox-coloured hair. Her hazel eyes found it hard to be still, and one hand stroked the fingers of the other.

"You are a miracle," said Arkona. "We are all miracles. When we start to seek sight and not spectacle we start to understand the vastness of the miracles by which we are surrounded. The grass you're sitting on, that is a miracle. The fact that each blade of it is different. All life is a miracle.

"So is life itself.

"The life-force, the existence, even the possibility of life.

"There are many scientists, many physicists who claim to be atheist and yet remain in awe of this life-force. Doctors who fight with all of their being to sustain life and who take it as a personal insult if they lose that fight. There can be no God, they argue, because God would not allow such cruelty.

"That is the argument not of the atheist, but of

those who allow others to define God for them.

"Is there not the divine lurking in such thinking? There is nothing physical, nothing palpable in it. It is just that: thinking. What is the difference between the abstract and the metaphysical?

"If the composer torches the manuscript paper, does that mean the symphony he had penned was not miraculous?

"The thing that angers so many of us about God is that we are not It. We are seized by the obviousness of it all: Children, we know, should not be allowed to die; injustice should not be allowed triumph. Why can't God see that?

"Mr Rolls designed cars. Is Mr Rolls responsible for the way people drive them?

"Flowers do not germinate by themselves. Is the bee's choice of nectar its own or God's? Is the shower that nurtures the flowers physical or metaphysical? How much of either? Do we try to assign roles to the various raindrops that fall on an individual bloom? It was the fourteenth raindrop that caused it life?

"I was," said the prophet, "brought back from the dead. A divine force, I have no doubt of it, returned me. For all that that return was effected by medical expertise and technological wizardry, it was a miracle quite as great as that which returned Lazarus. Because, as well as by the scientific process, it was effected by the love and the prayers of those who knew me and prayed for me. It was effected too by many I did not know, but whose hearts were so big they were able to pray for me also.

"Who is to say which part of that divine force was responsible for my return?

"Who is to say whether that force were manifested in thoughts and in love and in prayers, or whether it were manifested in the skill and dedication of those thousands involved directly and indirectly in the operation which saved me?

"The victims of Burke and Hare helped to save me. The man who first sharpened flint into a tool. Is there not already the divine at work here?

"Because not everyone can be loved back to life does not mean that none can. Nor does it mean that those who die are loved less than those who are resurrected.

"We look at a human being. Do we see its zillion parts?

"We tread on a spider, or squash a bug. We have destroyed a miracle of engineering infinitely more sophisticated than anything man has made. Do we look at a cockroach and see a miracle?

"Only man, the materialists maintain, can create miracles. Landing on the moon is a miracle. That the moon is there to be landed on is just a happenstance of fate.

"The chances of life even happening are so

enormous as to defy representation. We wonder though at a mobile phone and not the radiation from planets scores of light years away.

"If we realised fully the miracle of life, would be so casual with it?

"Go into the quiet. Let the quiet define for you what is truly a miracle, and what is merely cleverness.

"If we start to respect sight above spectacle we will start to save our lives."

•••

A dour young man clambered atop a rock. He wore glasses behind which grey eyes furrowed with intensity and an over-earnestness. "Talk to us about ambition," he said. Arkona loved him for his concern and hoped for him that laughter too would furrow those eyes.

"One of the few wise men of the twentieth century defined humankind's challenge as selling the world on love.

"We have to sell the world on love. That is not a luxury, but – if we are to survive – an obligation.

"Unless to love is our first ambition, and to sell that love is our second, we will have allowed Armageddon.

"In Armageddon the moneyed and frugal will die alongside the impoverished and prodigal, the obese alongside the starving, the generous with the avaricious, the vicious with the kind – the young, sadly, with the old. The innocent with the guilty.

"The world no longer has ambition for itself. It

is rotating in a vortex whirring with greed, lacking any direction beyond the illusion of self-interest.

"It is so blinkered, it is not even the self-interest of the infant in its crib.

"Unless we start caring for each other there will be no more world.

"Greed is not good. Greed is very bad. It is poisonous. Greed damages physical health and emotional health, spiritual and mental. Greed, as I have said before, is hatred. For your spiritual health it is another anthrax. Those who advocate greed are inviting you to commit spiritual hara-kiri.

"Go into the quiet. Look at those who preach such venom. Are they people you would listen to on your deathbed? Live listening only to those you would listen to on your deathbed.

"Listen to the quiet. Your quiet. Hear it. Heed it.

"There is nothing wrong with ambition. Ambition hauled humankind out of the sea. Ambition procreated the species.

"It is only distorted ambition which is wrong. Just as 'family' is not hurtful, only dysfunctional family.

"If you see your life as separate from all life you will distort ambition. If your ambition is to beat others your ambition is distorted. You achieve only if you achieve in conjunction with others. Even the painter cannot work without the paint manufacturer and the brush-maker. Those who seek to best others only worst themselves.

"Because finally they destroy the community which harbours them.

"Who do you want to see in an emergency? A stock-broker or a paramedic?

"Prime Ministers are not successful. They are power addicts. And, like any addict, their addiction warps them. Like any addict they are to be pitied.

"Plutocrats are not winners. They are money addicts. Like any addict they cannot have enough of the drug of their choice. Like any addict they are hugely disruptive of the community around them, and are selfish to the point of mania. Like any addict they too are to be pitied.

"Those who are successful are mostly those you have never heard of. And they are successful because they don't need to be heard of. They have the validation they need. They do not need the approbation and the plastic acclaim of others to feel themselves complete.

"They love themselves. Thus they love you. And me. And us. They love the planet. And they love life.

"Their words are distorted by a plutocratic press, and their deeds misrepresented by a delinquent Executive.

"Their protest is broadcast as violence, their outrage as criminal.

"It is the sane portrayed as the demented."

•••

THERE was a young woman in the crowd of fashionable curves and expensive sun-glasses. Her hair was groomed with the finest lotions and frankincense tripped from her as she walked. She looked coyly on the prophet, knowing she would distract many from his gaze. Usually she wore her celebrity more fluently. Today she felt inhibited. "Is not fame a fine thing?" she asked.

"My boat approaches the harbour," Arkona said. "I must make my way towards it. Walk with me," he invited.

"Fame," said the prophet as he walked, "is very rarely spontaneous. Usually it is produced. Either by the self or by others.

"If by the self, we are being asked to laud the egomaniac. If by others, the famous are no more significant than a packet of famous soap powder.

"It is only when the famous start to consider themselves more significant than soap powder that they become menacing.

"It is when they think their fame equals their goodness or their importance that they start harming themselves. It is when they think their fame entitles them to treat those not famous with anything other than respect that it becomes toxic.

"The biggest problem with fame is that it is so often manufactured for those who cannot cope with it.

"Fame is not a reward but a penalty. But those whose fame is constructed for them are usually too naïve to understand the blueprint and too blinded by their own self-importance to see the final edifice.

"Those of us who hanker for fame are probably still seeking the approval we failed to receive in childhood.

"Humankind needs the famous. They need you," he told the sun-glassed woman. "We have to love. We have also to idolise. Just as we need our pantheon, we need our demi-gods.

"We just choose those demi-gods so unwisely. As with our appreciation of the miraculous, we allow the specious to oust the special. We idolise sportspeople and singers and actors. The politicians and moguls insist we idolatrise moguls and politicians. It is such a waste of veneration.

"It is like drinking champagne now gone flat, or eating oysters that have been allowed to go rancid.

"There are – of course there are – human beings alive today worthy of respect. But they are all people.

They are not gods, not even demi-gods. There are those whose divinity, certainly, is greater than that of most of us. But that is only because they have had the courage to delve for it and to find it.

"We can admire our singers and our actors, even our sportspeople. But we do not need admiration to be manipulated into idolatry. There are few surer ways of guaranteeing that the values of tomorrow will be warped.

"And we can reserve contempt for those who purport to honour the young and to cherish the young and who use their fame to encourage those young to eat food which is harmful to them, or to drink synthetic liquids which rot their teeth and inhibit their brain.

"This is Herod gooing at babies as his henchmen plunge in the sword."

"Oh," said Saskja, "really, really angry." Arkona could not even raise a smile in her direction. "Really, really, *really* angry," said the little girl.

•••

"EVEN sportspeople?" asked a track-suited man. Beads of sweat were wobbling around his eyebrows. A stop-watch dangled from a dark green cord around his neck. There was a spring in his well-soled step, but a sad listlessness around his eyes. He bounced whilst the others trekked down the hill to the port.

"Sport today is not about creating winners," said Arkona, "but losers. There is much more disappointment in sport than there is jubilation. The smile of the gold-medallist costs how many tears?

"Friendly activities do not involve tears; character-building is not the task of industry. Sport is no longer about competition, but about making money. It is enormously divisive. And growing in its unhealthiness. It gives out entirely the wrong message. It tells the world, if the great 'I' can score more goals than you I am a better person than you. It tells the world, the world is a better place for the triumph of 'I'.

"The world now needs to hear – needs desperately to hear – that 'we' can do what 'I' can't.

That what 'I' can do is next to nothing. 'I' can't build a house or perform a medical operation. 'I' can milk a cow, but only 'we' can have it ready for me to pour into my morning coffee. 'I' can't even record a song or produce a film.

"Sport is no longer challenge but trade. And trade wants to create its demi-gods because demi-gods help them sell their over-priced wares. Even in team-matches today they award a 'Man of the Match' trophy. This doesn't encourage our children to play within a team, but to seek the limelight.

"Those who first climbed Everest wanted not to be drawn on who arrived first at the summit. It was irrelevant. It was a warped Press which demanded a 'winner'.

"Demi-gods sell newspapers.

"There is beauty in the human form honed to peak performance. There is grace in the movement of great athletes. Yet more, though, in great dancers.

"But that there is divinity at work in such movement does not mean that this is divinity.

"It is no longer religion which is the opiate of the masses, it is sport. It is used by the noise-makers to divert our attention from what is really important.

"It is silliness posturing as significance.

"It is the unhealthy hiding in the skirts of the healthy."

●●●

THEY were by now walking down the cobbled streets on the fringes of the town. These were the slums of Orphalese. They smelt of rotting vegetables and an overall decay.

The prophet's energy was not that of his youth. He stopped now to gather his thoughts and a second wind.

"You are not well?" asked a nurse, her blue eyes blueing darker in her concern.

"I am a man," said Arkona. "And I am old."

"You are not old," Lakshmi rejoindered quickly. "And because you are a man, your pains seem greater than they are."

They smiled together. A part of their bond was humour. A part was very earthly.

"Talk to us," the nurse said, "of sickness and of health."

"Doctors are today realising what the enlightened have known for centuries: that it is the whole body, the whole spirit contained by that body, which needs treatment and not that part of the body alone which appears to be suffering. So often the apparent ailment is only the symptom.

"Mental and emotional imbalance causes physical imbalance. Spiritual imbalance impairs all three.

"All of us are sick some of the time, and some of us are sick all of the time. And the sickest of all amongst us are those who think they are not sick.

"Some of the worst ailments are those which tell you you do not have them.

"How much more sick the bursar refusing to pay for treatment than the patient thus deprived.

"The man who runs a weekly marathon and screams regularly at his children is not healthy.

"The woman who eats a fat-free diet but cannot sleep without pills is not healthy.

"You're going to ask why, if that is the case, so many of the spiritually delinquent – the senators and moguls – attain a robust longevity. I don't know. My quiet does not know. It is simply a conundrum. There *are* conundra in this world. Just as there are paradoxes. There always will be both. Even in Utopia. Let us rejoice in them.

"It may be such a conundrum also keeping *us* alive.

"Can any of us really be healthy living on such an unhealthy planet?

"Should we not start applying the lessons that medicine has taught us to the welfare also of the planet?

"Medicine teaches us, sometimes if our back is hurting, it is our teeth which need attention.

"Acupuncture teaches us that pressure points in the feet can affect organs an entire body away.

"Anatomy teaches us that toes and ears belong to the same body.

"The North and South Poles belong too to the same body, Timbuktu and Tibet, Japan and New Jersey.

"But we do not get our toes syringed nor clip our earnails. We can know each part of our body is one of a whole, yet respect each part also for itself. Let each part of the body *be* its own part. The body is not improved by the liver insisting all other organs become liverlike.

"I must walk on. Walk with me," Arkona smiled.

"I choke on the sadness I have in leaving you," Arkona said. "You are beautiful people, you people of Orphalese.

"The world's people, people of Orphalese, are beautiful, beautiful people.

"They deserve better than to witness a possible Eden turned into a cesspit, the promise of paradise sold for the guarantee of purgatory.

"And at what price?

"So that a handful of the already incalculably rich can become still richer.

"You ask me to talk of sickness and of health. Already the living on this planet is demanding a heavy compromise in our health. If we do not – and very soon – reverse most of the directions we are taking, it will become a requirement to live on this planet that we are unhealthy.

"Spiritually, that possibility is obvious.

"Emotionally and mentally we will soon start having to do such ethical cartwheels that we will spend our lives perpetually giddy.

"Physically ... the evidence is all about us.

"We allow fast food chains to 'sponsor' health pavilions, and Cola companies to 'sponsor' schools.

"The same doublethink would have our hospitals sponsored by tobacco companies.

"We know an unbalanced diet can lead to social delinquency. And yet we send our young offenders to reform schools rather than change their diets.

"Pain is there for a reason.

"Pain tells us there's something wrong. Please tend to it.

"Go into the quiet. Hear the screams of the planet's torment. Hear it. Heed it.

"Do not listen to the noise-makers, those who would have you believe that as each year progresses so the world is a better place to live in. They contend that it is better because we have better toys to play with.

"Toys only make the crib a more fun place to be in. Do you want to remain an infant? Do you want to remain penned behind bars?

"We take responsibility for our physical health when we eat properly and exercise and take sufficient breaks.

"We take responsibility for our emotional and mental health when we listen to the noise-makers with scepticism, when we go regularly into the quiet, and when we talk regularly with people safe for us to talk to.

"Our spiritual health requires us only sometimes to be quiet and always to be kind.

"Our whole health, though, requires a healthy planet. Go into the quiet. Sieve out the lies. Listen not to me. Listen to your own quiet.

"The wealthiest earn over a thousand dollars a second. Every second. Every day. In the time it has taken me to say the words they have earned a thousand dollars more. And there another.

"In that time a child has died from malnourishment or a want of proper medicine. Another school-book has fallen apart that will not be replaced, one child has been beaten, another sexually abused.

"We do the world's health a huge favour when we take care of our own.

"But to try and tackle the world's illnesses and dis-eases without also addressing the economic disparity would be to treat the obesity of a heart sufferer by shaving him. He may well need a shave but it is not going to tackle the central problem.

"Let us all recognise that, yes, we are all whole (or can work to become whole). We are all separate. But we are all, all of us, as well part of a larger whole.

"Whilst the whole cannot be healthy before I can, it is also true that I cannot be well until the whole is well.

"As well as for my own wholeness, therefore, I also need to work for the wholeness of the whole."

They had arrived by now at the harbour. Gulls cawed overhead, flotsam bobbed on gentle waves. The tang of fish and ozone savouried the air. He kissed those of the throng that wanted kissing, and hugged those who wanted hugs – and embraced with his soul those who wanted neither.

Saskja he squatted before. He gazed at her long and lovingly. And then he kissed her and squashed her nose with his finger.

Lakshmi he said goodbye to last of all. He kissed her almost brusquely, hugged her almost too hard.

"You talked earlier of triumph," she said. "But what of success?"

"I cannot give you the secret of success," he said. "If it is a secret to be given it is one only your own quiet can give you. But I can give you the secret both to failure and disaster: to imagine the world's dis-ease will somehow sort itself out, or that the spiritual delinquents now in control of it will sort it out.

"Greed in devouring everything has to end by devouring itself. You it will have devoured long beforehand.

"I love you all. But I must go. I, Arkona, will not be back. If there is a future – if you, people of Orphalese, are courageous enough to wrest a future from its pyre – then another will be back. Whether that will be Almustafa or I or a part of one or a part of both or an independent third, that will be for your successors individually in their own quiet to determine.

"There will never be a life without tragedy. There will never be a life where kindness is not at a premium. Can we not start creating a life where hope is not the privilege of the affluent, but a resource available to us all? Where there is, at least, a hope of hope?

"Citizens of Orphalese, I ask God to bless you. Please remember to bless yourselves."

••• *The End* •••

O

is a symbol of the world,
of oneness and unity. O Books
explores the many paths of wholeness
and spiritual understanding which
different traditions have developed down
the ages. It aims to bring this knowledge
in accessible form, to a general readership,
providing practical spirituality to today's seekers.
For the full list of over 200 titles covering:

- CHILDREN'S PRAYER, NOVELTY AND GIFT BOOKS
- CHILDREN'S CHRISTIAN AND SPIRITUALITY
- CHRISTMAS AND EASTER
- RELIGION/PHILOSOPHY
- SCHOOL TITLES
- ANGELS/CHANNELLING
- HEALING/MEDITATION
- SELF-HELP/RELATIONSHIPS
- ASTROLOGY/NUMEROLOGY
- SPIRITUAL ENQUIRY
- CHRISTIANITY, EVANGELICAL
AND LIBERAL/RADICAL
- CURRENT AFFAIRS
- HISTORY/BIOGRAPHY
- INSPIRATIONAL/DEVOTIONAL
- WORLD RELIGIONS/INTERFAITH
- BIOGRAPHY AND FICTION
- BIBLE AND REFERENCE
- SCIENCE/PSYCHOLOGY

Please visit our website,
www.O-books.net

Some recent O Books

TORN CLOUDS
Judy Hall

Drawing on thirty years experience as a regression therapist and her own memories and experiences in Egypt, ancient and modern, *Torn Clouds* is a remarkable first novel by an internationally-acclaimed MBS author, one of Britain's leading experts on reincarnation. It features time-traveller Megan McKennar, whose past life memories thrust themselves into the present day as she traces a love affair that transcends time. Haunted by her dreams, she is driven by forces she cannot understand to take a trip to Egypt in a quest to understand the cause of her unhappy current life circumstances. Once there, swooning into a previous existence in Pharaonic Egypt, she lives again as Meck'an'ar, priestess of the Goddess Sekhmet, the fearful lion headed deity who was simultaneously the Goddess of Terror, Magic and Healing.

Caught up in the dark historical secrets of Egypt, Megan is forced to fight for her soul. She succeeds in breaking the curse that had been cast upon her in two incarnations.

Judy Hall is a modern seer who manages the difficult task of evoking the present world, plus the realm of Ancient Egypt, and making them seem real. There is an energy behind the prose, and a power in her imagery which hints that this is more than just a story of character and plot, but an outpouring from another age, a genuine glimpse into beyond-time Mysteries which affect us all today. Alan Richardson, author of *Inner Guide to Egypt.*

Judy Hall has been a karmic counsellor for thirty years. Her books have been translated into over fourteen languages.

1 903816 80 7
£9.99/$14.95

THE QUEST
Joycelin Dawes

What is your sense of soul? Although we may each understand the word differently, we treasure a sense of who we are, what it is to be alive and awareness of an inner experience and connection with "something more." In *The Quest* you explore this sense of soul through a regular practice based on skills of spiritual reflection and be reviewing the story of your life journey, your encounter with spiritual experience and your efforts to live in a sacred way.

Here you become the teller and explorer of your own story. You can find your own answers. You can deepen your spiritual life through the wisdom and insight of the world's religious traditions. You can revisit the building blocks of your beliefs and face the changes in your life. You can look more deeply at wholeness and connection and make your contribution to finding a new and better way.

So well written, constructed and presented, by a small independent group of individuals with many years experience in personal and spiritual growth, education and community, that it is a joy to work with. It is a life-long companion on the spiritual path and an outstanding achievement; it is a labour of love, created with love to bring more love into our world. Susanna Michaelis, *Caduceus*

1 903816 93 9
£9.99/$16.95

JOURNEY HOME
Tonika Rinar

Tonika Rinar believes that everybody is capable of time travel. We can access history as it really happened, without later exaggeration or bias. We can also heal ourselves by coming to terms with our experiences in past lives.

Tonika escorts the reader into other worlds and dimensions, explaining her own remarkable experiences with an easy-to-read approach. At one level the book can simply be taken as a series of fascinating experiences with the paranormal, embracing past life regression, ghosts, angels and spirit guides. But it also encourages the reader along their own journey of self-discovery and understanding. A journey in which you can discover your own connection with the Universe and the many different dimensions contained within Creation.

Journey Home offers a multitude of insights, and along the way looks at some of the fundamental questions asked by all cultures around the world. Where do we come from? Why are we here? What is the point of our life? What happens when we die?

Tonika Rinar is an extraordinary psychic and visionary, international speaker and workshop leader, with 17 years clinical experience in working with people suffering injury and illness. She has been interviewed extensively on radio and TV.

1 905047 00 2
£11.99 $16.95

THE VISION
Out-of-body revelations of divine wisdom
Jaap Hiddinga

Visions and out-of-body experiences are not uncommon, but few have been experienced in such depth, and articulated with such clarity, as those of *Jaap Hildinga*. He began to have them as a young child, and out of the thousands he has accumulated since then he presents here some of the most powerful. They range from the Christ awareness that came into the world at the birth of Jesus to travels in other dimensions, in other times, in this universe and beyond. Along the way he raises questions and suggests answers about the origins of Christianity, the nature of the quantum world, the links between the earthly and spiritual worlds, and the future of humanity

Jaap Hildinga offers no particular interpretation or path to wisdom. It is not a book on how to travel out of the body, but a record of what one person was shown when he did so. The visions are recorded as they were received. As he says, each individual can take from it what they want or need. His conviction is that they can be of value to other searchers. They changed his life, maybe they can change yours. They point to a universe that is lovingly shepherding humanity to a future that at present it can barely dream of.

Jaap Hildinga studied chemistry at university and set up a petrochemical engineering firm at Falkirk in Scotland, where he has lived for the last twenty years. In 1993 he had a revelation that completely changed his thinking and his way of life. He sold the company he had set up, and is now an independent advisor for management and export marketing.

£9.99/$14.95
1 905047 05 3

THE SECRET JOURNEY
Poems and prayers from around the world
Susan Skinner

A gift book for the young in heart and spirit

These prayers, verses and invocations are drawn from many faiths and many nations but they all reflect the same mystery: the mystery our passage from birth, through life, to death. We are born from the unknown. Our life, except perhaps to our friends and family, is a secret journey of joy and sorrow. Our death is shrouded in questions.

In the words of St Paul, "now we see through a glass darkly.." But we *do* see some things, if we respond to the spirit within. Most faiths, personal or communal, acknowledge the inspiration of the spiritual life founded on truth, love and compassion.

This anthology is a small reflection of the inspired and enlightening words that have been passed on down the centuries, throughout the world. They sing to the child within us all, to the spirit which always remains open and free and clear-sighted. In the words of Master Eckhart: "The eye with which I see God is the same eye with which God sees me."

Each reflection is stunningly illustrated in full colour, making this an ideal gift book for the young and anyone starting on the spiritual journey, or seeking images and verses for inspiration and meditation. A map and short introduction to the world religions, along with notes on sources, make it a useful addition to all libraries in homes and schools.

Susan Skinner is an artist who has made a life long study of world religions, working their themes into exquisite images. She lives near Hastings, England.

1 905047 08 8
£11.99/$16.95

HEALING HANDS
David Vennells

Hand reflexology is one of the most well-known and respected complementary therapies, practised in many hospitals, surgeries, hospices, health and healing centres, and is enjoying a growing popularity. *Healing Hands* explains the simple techniques of Hand Reflexology so clearly, with the aid of illustrations, that "within a few days the reader could be competently treating themselves or others." It is aimed at those interested in learning the practical techniques (how to give yourself and others a full treatment), and also includes the fascinating history of reflexology, how it works with the hands and the various things we can do to support the healing process. As the reader learns the techniques step by step, they can gradually increase their knowledge of anatomy and physiology, together with developing a more accurate awareness of the hand reflexes and how to treat them accurately and successfully.

David Vennells is a Buddhist teacher of Reiki and the author of *Reiki Mastery* (O Books).
1 903816 81 5
£9.99/$16.95

REIKI MASTERY
For Second Degree Students and Masters
David Vennells

Reiki has many levels and forms, and has changed along the way from the pure, "original" practice of its Buddhist founder, Dr. Mikao Usui. Advanced Reiki, especially above First Degree, is about "facing the mirror," the inner mirror of our own mind. As we progress with our spiritual practice we can begin to clean away the layers of misconception that colour the way we view ourselves, others and the world around us. This is a compassionate, wise, handbook to making the most of the Life Force Energy that surrounds and informs us all.

David Vennells is a Buddhist teacher of Reiki and the author of *Reiki for Beginners, Bach Flower Remedies for Beginners, Reflexology for Beginners.*

1-903816-70-X
£9.99 $14.95